OTHER PASSPORTS

Other Passports

POEMS 1958–1985

Clive James

JONATHAN CAPE
THIRTY-TWO BEDFORD SQUARE
LONDON

This collection first published 1986
This collection copyright © 1986 by Clive James
Individual poems copyright © to the year listed before their page number:
1961, p. 127; 1965, p. 132; 1966, pp. 50, 129, 134, 135, 138; 1968, p. 136;
1972, pp. 69, 77, 85, 92, 99, 103, 141; 1973, pp. 43, 46, 49, 54, 55, 58, 63;
1974, pp. 60, 64, 142; 1976, p. 51; 1977, p. 143; 1978, p. 45; 1980, pp. 8, 11, 122;
1981, pp. 114, 149; 1982, p. 56; 1983, pp. 3, 163; 1984, pp. 9, 12, 14, 16, 20, 21,
24, 29; 1985, p. 5; 1986, pp. 18, 26, 28, 35, 54, 119, 128, 130, 131, 144

Jonathan Cape Ltd, 32 Bedford Square, London WC1B 3EL

British Library Cataloguing in Publication Data

James, Clive
Other passports : poems 1958–1985
I. Title
821   PR9619.3.J27

ISBN 0-224-02422-1

Typeset by Columns of Reading
Printed by The Alden Press
Osney Mead, Oxford

To Karl Miller

Contents

Acknowledgments

Acknowledgments are due to the editors of *Encounter*, the *Listener*, the *London Review of Books*, the *New Review*, the *New Statesman*, the *Observer* and the *Times Literary Supplement*, in which some of these poems first appeared.

Some of the earlier poems appeared in the Sydney University magazines *Arna*, *Hermes* and *Pluralist*; *Melbourne University Magazine*; and the Cambridge University magazines *Carcanet*, *Inverse*, *Granta*, *Pawn* and *Solstice*.

Some poems have been anthologised in *Young Commonwealth Poets '65*, edited by P. L. Brent; *New Poems, 1971–1972*, edited by Peter Porter; *New Poems 1972–1973*, edited by Douglas Dunn; *Anthology of Contemporary Poetry*, edited by John Wain; *Brand X Poetry*, edited by William Zaranka; *The Faber Book of Parodies*, edited by Simon Brett; *The Oxford Book of Satirical Verse*, edited by Geoffrey Grigson; *The Penguin Australian Book of Satirical Verse*, edited by Philip Neilsen; and *The New Oxford Book of Australian Verse*, edited by Les A. Murray.

Introduction

During thirty years of writing verse, one hopes to have improved, but can only have done so by becoming more self-critical, a development which tends to winnow the crop in advance of the harvest. Therefore I am pleased to find some things asking to be kept even from early on. If it does not sound too grand to say that there was an initial phase, it was the ten-year period in which I wrote what were meant to be lyric poems. These mainly went into university magazines and newspapers either in Sydney or in Cambridge, and in the pages of those publications most of them demand to lie undisturbed. Though I never had what it took to be obscure, clarity still had to be worked for. Local outbreaks of straightforwardness from the early part of this struggle are here preserved under the title 'Earlier Verse', not because I want to disown them but because even at their most transparent they try so hard to disown me. To write in his own voice is every poet's object, and my voice, I have since realised, was the prosaic one I speak with. It was so close to hand that it took an age to reach.

A big help along the way was a second phase, not represented here. At Cambridge I began writing song lyrics for the music of my fellow undergraduate, Pete Atkin. In the next eight years we published half a dozen record albums. I never wrote from a surer instinct. But there came a point, while I was still writing song lyrics, when another instinct awkwardly insisted that I was not yet quite through with writing verse. The awkwardness lay in the fact that the new urge was theatrical. Having my song lyrics performed had given me a taste for going public. My mock epic poem *Peregrine Prykke's Pilgrimage* was the brazen outcome. Eventually it had three successors, and all four mock epics might one day appear together in a single volume suitably annotated, but here I need only say that before attempting that first, long, parodic poem-for-performance I wrote a number of isolated parodies, imitations and lampoons, most of which were first published under the name of Edward Pygge.

Hard news about Edward Pygge might prove useful to those

[xi]

scholars who concern themselves with the London Literary World in its more subterranean aspects. Pygge's activities were designedly shrouded in mystery, but by now there is a new generation of *literati* on the scene to whom the mystery looks like a conspiracy. It never was. Pygge simply happened. In his heyday he was three people. Ian Hamilton invented him, and composed, mainly for the pages of that astringent little magazine *The Review*, his first withering attacks on current poetic fashion. My own additions to the swinish canon were made in order to generate more material for a one-night literary spectacular presented at the ICA in the Mall. Rehearsed irregularly at the Pillars of Hercules in Greek Street, Soho, and unofficially known as the Edward Pygge Revue, the show was produced by Hamilton and myself but stolen outright by Russell Davies, who made a dramatic, unheralded appearance in the role of Pygge. Seemingly just off a plane from Chicago, Davies wore a dark suit, darker shirt, white tie, pointed shoes, and a black fedora with the brim pulled low over the eyes. He carried a violin case under his arm as if it contained a Thompson sub-machine gun loaded ready for action. He read our Pygge poems in a variety of voices to stunning effect. It should also be said that his own Pygge poems, when he could be persuaded to write them, were of deadly accuracy and unmatched inventiveness. He had that flair. The last two lines of 'The Wasted Land', for example, were supplied by Davies *sotto voce*, or perhaps *blotto voce*, as he sipped a pint at rehearsal. I appropriated them without compunction.

A man to respect, a back-room boy, an itinerant torpedo whose power depended on the obscurity of his turned-up coat collar, Edward Pygge found his reputation turning into fame, with all of its attendant dangers. On two occasions there were double-page spreads of Pygge poems in the *New Statesman*. Pygge started showing up in the same paper's weekly competition. He became a handy sobriquet for anyone who had a spoof to launch. The feminist termagant Edwina Pygge put in an appearance. Obviously it would have been only a matter of time before Edward and Edwina were joined by Kedward Pygge and their Nordic cousin, Hedwig Pygge. The star having gone nova, he duly dissipated into a nebula. Occupied by long confections far out of scale with Pygge's pin-point focus, I forgot that I had ever been part of the collective brain beneath that dangerously angled black hat.

As well as the mock epics which are not here, I wrote verse letters which are. The first seven of these were published in book form under the title *Fan-Mail*, a term which Philip Larkin, in a letter, correctly pointed out should not have a hyphen. A slim volume verging on the flimsy, it was reviewed like the plague but did me good. The different verse forms I adopted were identical in their salutary discipline. It sounds like masochism and sometimes felt like it, but in the long run the exigencies of rhyme and metre made plainness mandatory by revealing would-be profundities as fudge. Here I have felt bound to discard only the first verse letter I wrote. Addressed to John Fuller, it was too clumsy to keep, in view of the high standards of craftsmanship he has set for those poets of his generation who have followed his example in producing, or trying to produce, urbane and entertaining public verse.

The only other things I have subtracted from the *Fan-Mail* verse letters are the italicisation, extra capital letters and cognate olde worlde furniture which excused them as a deliberate throwback, when I should have admitted that I meant every word of them. I have included two verse letters written less apologetically later on, the ones to Michael Frayn and Craig Raine, and in the same section put two birthday poems, for Anthony Thwaite and Gore Vidal. This whole intermediate phase of extended rhyme-scheming was rounded out, symbolically if not chronologically, by my fourth mock epic *Charles Charming's Challenges*, for which the West End critics demanded that its perpetrator be transported to Botany Bay, and were not to be mollified by the information that he was born there. Adopting a new disguise as a novelist, I discreetly vacated the poetic scene.

While hiding out through a long winter, I remembered Pygge. Having found a legitimate freedom of language through strict form, I was ready to recapture, *in propria persona* this time, my share of Pygge's laconic anarchy, his mimetic disdain, his heroic disinclination to be impressed. It occurred to me that the poems I had written under his name were the first that had been entirely mine – the reason that I reproduce them here, minus the porcine pseudonym. A strange characteristic of

[xiii]

parody is that by tightening your grip on someone else's throat you can loosen your own tongue. Pygge would pitch his voice at any level that suited the case, shade it to any tone. Either he trusted his own personality to come through anyway or else he simply didn't give a damn. Now that he had finished copying everybody else, I resolved to copy him.

The shorter pieces grouped under the heading 'Recent Verse' were composed in the euphoria of this very elementary breakthrough. Taking strict form from my longer poems and polyphonic courage from Pygge, I wrote them in matching stanzas when the occasion demanded, and free verse when it did not. But the freedom would not have been the same without the discipline, nor the discipline without the freedom. In the compound of those two elements resides the only concept of the modern that I am willing to understand. Recent verse is a category which I hope I will go on adding to for the rest of my life. It turned out, however, that the urge to write longer poems was not extinct, merely dormant. They rose again in the form of verse diaries. 'An Address to the Nation' was the rehearsal for *Poem of the Year*. I include them both here, without the author's note attached to the latter when it was first printed in book form. If these two verse diaries seem to take up a disproportionate space, it doesn't mean that I value long poems more than short ones. But I don't value them less, either. At any length, the aim is brevity.

London, 1986

Recent Verse

The Book of My Enemy Has Been Remaindered

The book of my enemy has been remaindered
And I am pleased.
In vast quantities it has been remaindered.
Like a van-load of counterfeit that has been seized
And sits in piles in a police warehouse,
My enemy's much-praised effort sits in piles
In the kind of bookshop where remaindering occurs.
Great, square stacks of rejected books and, between them, aisles
One passes down reflecting on life's vanities,
Pausing to remember all those thoughtful reviews
Lavished to no avail upon one's enemy's book –
For behold, here is that book
Among these ranks and banks of duds,
These ponderous and seemingly irreducible cairns
Of complete stiffs.

The book of my enemy has been remaindered
And I rejoice.
It has gone with bowed head like a defeated legion
Beneath the yoke.
What avail him now his awards and prizes,
The praise expended upon his meticulous technique,
His individual new voice?
Knocked into the middle of next week
His brainchild now consorts with the bad buys,
The sinkers, clinkers, dogs and dregs,
The Edsels of the world of movable type,
The bummers that no amount of hype could shift,
The unbudgeable turkeys.

Yea, his slim volume with its understated wrapper
Bathes in the glare of the brightly jacketed *Hitler's War
    Machine*,
His unmistakably individual new voice
Shares the same scrapyard with a forlorn skyscraper
Of *The Kung-Fu Cookbook*,

His honesty, proclaimed by himself and believed in by others,
His renowned abhorrence of all posturing and pretence,
Is there with *Pertwee's Promenades and Pierrots* –
One Hundred Years of Seaside Entertainment,
And (oh, this above all) his sensibility,
His sensibility and its hair-like filaments,
His delicate, quivering sensibility is now as one
With *Barbara Windsor's Book of Boobs,*
A volume graced by the descriptive rubric
'My boobs will give everyone hours of fun.'

Soon now a book of mine could be remaindered also,
Though not to the monumental extent
In which the chastisement of remaindering has been meted out
To the book of my enemy,
Since in the case of my own book it will be due
To a miscalculated print run, a marketing error –
Nothing to do with merit.
But just supposing that such an event should hold
Some slight element of sadness, it will be offset
By the memory of this sweet moment.
Chill the champagne and polish the crystal goblets!
The book of my enemy has been remaindered
And I am glad.

Sack Artist

Reeling between the redhead and the blonde
Don Juan caught the eye of the brunette.
He had no special mission like James Bond.
He didn't play the lute or read *Le Monde*.
Why was it he on whom their sights were set?

For let's make no mistake, the women pick
Which men go down in history as avid
Tail-chasers with the enviable trick
Of barely needing to chat up the chick –
From Warren Beatty back to ruddy David.

But why the broads latch on to the one bloke
Remains what it has always been, a riddle.
Byron though famous was both fat and broke
While Casanova was a standing joke,
His wig awry, forever on the fiddle.

Mozart made Juan warble but so what?
In *Don Giovanni* everybody sings.
The show would fall flat if the star did not
And clearly he's not meant to sound so hot:
His women praise him, but for other things.

They trill of his indifference and disdain
But might have liked his loyalty still more.
We can't, from how they lyrically complain,
Conclude that when he left they liked the pain
As much as they enjoyed the bliss before.

Bad treatment doesn't do it: not from him,
Still less from us, who find out when we try it
That far from looking tickled they turn grim,
Leaving us at a loss out on a limb,
Instructed to obtain a kite and fly it.

Which doesn't make the chap of whom we speak
Some gigolo devoted to their pleasure.
The fancy man turns no strong woman weak
But merely pumps out what was up the creek.
Plundering hulks he lays up little treasure.

Good looks don't hurt but rate low on their own.
The teenage girls who fall for Richard Gere
Admit his face is random flesh and bone
Beside Mel Gibson's, that his skin lacks tone
And when he smiles his pin eyes disappear.

They go bananas when he bares his chest
But torsos that outstrip his leave them cold.
One bit of you might well be the world's best
But women won't take that and leave the rest:
The man entire is what they would enfold.

The phallus fallacy thus shows its roots
Afloat in the pornographer's wet dream
By which a synechdochal puss in boots
Strides forward frantic to be in cahoots
With his shy mote grown into a great beam.

A shame to be without the wherewithal
But all the wherewith you might have down there
Won't get the ladies queuing in the hall –
Not if you let it loose at a masked ball,
Not if you advertise it on the air.

None of which means that lust takes a back seat.
Contrariwise, it is the main event.
The grandest *grandes dames* cease to be discreet.
Their souls shine through their bodies with the heat.
They dream of more to come as they lie spent.

The sort of women who don't do such things
Do them for him, wherein might lie the clue.
The smell of transcendental sanction clings
Like injured ozone to angelic wings –
An envoy, and he's only passing through.

[6]

In triumph's moment he must hit the trail.
However warm the welcome, he can't stay.
Lest those fine fingers read his back like braille
He has to pull out early without fail –
Preserve his mystery with a getaway.

He is the perfect stranger. Humbler grades
Of female don't get even a brief taste –
With Errol Flynn fenced in by flashing blades
And Steve McQueen in aviator shades
It always was a dream that they embraced.

Sheer fantasy makes drama from the drab,
Sweet reverie a slow blues from the bleak:
How Cary Grant would not pick up the tab,
Omar Sharif sent roses in a cab,
Those little lumps in Robert Redford's cheek.

Where Don's concerned the first glance is enough:
For certain he takes soon what we might late.
The rest of us may talk seductive guff
Unendingly and not come up to snuff,
Whereat we most obscenely fulminate.

We say of her that she can't pass a prick.
We call him cunt-struck, stick-man, power tool,
Muff-diver, stud, sack artist, motor dick,
Getting his end away, dipping his wick,
A stoat, a goat, a freak, a fucking fool.

So we stand mesmerised by our own fuss,
Aware that any woman, heaped with grief,
Will give herself to him instead of us
Because there is so little to discuss –
And cry *perfido mostro*! in relief.

Her true desires at long last understood,
She ponders, as she holds him locked above her,
The living definition of the good –
Her blind faith in mankind and womanhood
Restored by the dumb smile of the great lover.

The Supreme Farewell of Handkerchiefs

With acknowledgments to Arthur Gold and Robert Fizdale, authors of Misia

'I've left that great page blank,' said Mallarmé
When asked why he'd not written of his boat.
There are such things as mean too much to say.
You have to let it drift, to let it float.

The man who did the asking was Manet,
Whose niece's journal treasures the reply.
There are such things as mean too much to say,
But little Julie Manet had a try.

To represent the young, Paul Valéry
Delivered half a speech and then broke down.
He missed his master's deep simplicity.
Then everybody started back to town.

Among those present were Rodin, Bonnard,
Lautrec, Mirbeau, Vallotton, Maeterlinck
And Misia's eternal slave Vuillard.
But Renoir, who had painted her in pink,

Knew ways to tame her when she got annoyed
At how they laughed instead of looking glum.
He thought such moments ought to be enjoyed.
Had not mortality been overcome?

Said Renoir, who had been the poet's friend:
'A Mallarmé does not die every day.'
A sly hint of his own approaching end?
There are such things as mean too much to say.
'I've left that great page blank,' said Mallarmé.

[8]

A Gesture towards James Joyce

My gesture towards Finnegans Wake *is deliberate.*
Ronald Bush, *T. S. Eliot: A Study in Character and Style*

The gesture towards *Finnegans Wake* was deliberate.
It was not accidental.
Years of training went into the gesture,
As W. C. Fields would practise a juggling routine
Until his eczema-prone hands bled in their kid gloves;
As Douglas Fairbanks Sr trimmed the legs of a table
Until, without apparent effort and from a standing start,
He could jump up on to it backwards;
Or as Gene Kelly danced an entire tracking shot over and over
Until the final knee-slide ended exactly in focus,
Loafers tucked pigeon-toed behind him,
Perfect smile exultant,
Hands thrown open saying 'How *about* that?'

The gesture towards *Finnegans Wake* was deliberate.
Something so elaborate could not have been otherwise.
Though an academic gesture, it partook in its final form
Of the balletic arabesque,
With one leg held out extended to the rear
And the equiponderant forefinger pointing demonstratively
Like the statue of Eros in Piccadilly Circus,
Or, more correctly, the Mercury of Giambologna,
Although fully, needless to say, clad.

The gesture towards *Finnegans Wake* was deliberate,
Its aim assisted by the position of the volume,
A 1957 printing in the yellow and orange wrapper
Propped on a sideboard and opened at page 164
So that the gesture might indicate a food-based conceit
About *pudding the carp before doeuvre hors* –
The Joycean amalgam in its ludic essence,
Accessible to students and yet also evincing
The virtue of requiring a good deal of commentary
Before what looked simple even if capricious
Emerged as precise even if complex
And ultimately unfathomable.

[9]

The gesture towards *Finnegans Wake* was deliberate,
Being preceded by an 'It is no accident, then',
An exuberant 'It is neither accidental nor surprising'
And at least two cases of 'It is not for nothing that',
These to adumbrate the eventual paroxysm
In the same way that a bouncer from Dennis Lillee
Has its overture of giant strides galumphing towards you
With the face both above and below the ridiculous moustache
Announcing by means of unmistakable grimaces
That what comes next is no mere spasm
But a premeditated attempt to knock your block off.

The gesture towards *Finnegans Wake* was deliberate
And so was my gesture with two fingers.
In America it would have been one finger only
But in Italy I might have employed both arms,
The left hand crossing to the tense right bicep
As my clenched fist jerked swiftly upwards –
The most deliberate of all gestures because most futile,
Defiantly conceding the lost battle.

The gesture towards *Finnegans Wake* was deliberate:
So much so that Joyce should have seen it coming
Even through the eye-patch of his last years.
He wrote a book full of nothing except writing
For people who can't do anything but read,
And now their gestures clog the air around us.
He asked for it, and we got it.

Thoughts on Feeling Carbon-Dated

No moons are left to see the other side of.
Curved surfaces betray once secret centres.
Those plagues were measles the Egyptians died of.
A certain note of disillusion enters.

Were Empson starting now, no doubt exists
That now no doubt exists about space-time's
Impetuosity his pithy gists
Would still stun, but no more so than his rhymes.

Physics has dished its prefix meta. Science,
First having put black shoes and a blue suit on,
Controls the world's supply of mental giants.
A Goethe now would lack words to loathe Newton.

It's forty years since James Joyce named the quark.
Now nobody's nonplussed to hear light rays
Get sucked down holes so fast they show up dark.
Nor would the converse of that news amaze.

It all gets out of reach as it grows clear.
What we once failed to grasp but still were thrilled with
Left us for someone else, from whom we hear
Assurances about the awe they're filled with.

One night in Cambridge Empson read to us.
He offered us some crisps and seemed delighted
So many young should still want to discuss
Why science once got laymen so excited.

Johnny Weissmuller Dead in Acapulco

Apart possibly from waving hello to the cliff-divers
Would the real Tarzan have ever touched Acapulco?
Not with a one-hundred-foot vine.
Jungle Jim maybe, but the Ape Man never.
They played a tape at his funeral
In the Valley of Light cemetery of how he had sounded
Almost fifty years back giving the pristine ape-call,
Which could only remind all present that in decline
He would wander distractedly in the garden
With his hands to his mouth and the unforgettable cry
Coming out like a croak –
This when he wasn't sitting in his swim-trunks
Beside the pool he couldn't enter without nurses.

Things had not been so bad before Mexico
But they were not great.
He was a greeter in Caesar's Palace like Joe Louis.
Sal, I want you should meet Johnny Weissmuller.
Johnny, Mr Sal Volatile is a friend of ours from Chicago.
With eighteen Tarzan movies behind him
Along with the five Olympic gold medals,
He had nothing in front except that irrepressible paunch
Which brought him down out of the tree house
To earth as Jungle Jim
So a safari suit could cover it up.
As Jungle Jim he wasn't just on salary,
He had a piece of the action,
But coming so late in the day it was not enough
And in Vegas only the smile was still intact.

As once it had all been intact, the Greek classic body
Unleashing the new-style front-up crawl like a baby
Lifting itself for the first time,
Going over the water almost as much as through it,
Curing itself of childhood polio
By making an aquaplane of its deep chest,

Each arm relaxing out of the water and stiffening into it,
The long legs kicking a trench that did not fill up
Until he came back on the next lap,
Invincible, easily breathing
The air in the spit-smooth, headlong, creek-around-a-rock
    trough
Carved by his features.

He had six wives like Henry VIII but don't laugh,
Because Henry VIII couldn't swim a stroke
And if you ever want to see a true king you should watch
    Weissmuller
In *Tarzan Escapes* cavorting underwater with Boy
In the clear river with networks of light on the shelving sand
Over which they fly weightless to hide from each other behind
    the log
While Jane wonders where they are.
You will wonder where you are too and be shy of the answer
Because it is Paradise.

When the crocodile made its inevitable entry into the clear river
Tarzan could always settle its hash with his bare hands
Or a knife at most,
But Jungle Jim usually had to shoot it
And later on he just never got to meet it face to face –
It was working for the Internal Revenue Service.

There was a chimpanzee at his funeral,
Which must have been someone's idea of a smart promotion,
And you might say dignity had fled,
But when Tarzan dropped from the tall tree and swam out of
    the splash
Like an otter with an outboard to save Boy from the waterfall
It looked like poetry to me,
And at home in the bath I would surface giving the ape-call.

Reflections on a Cardboard Box

Hostathion contains Triazophos,
Controls seed weevil, pea moth, carrot fly.
Of pesticides Hostathion is the boss.
Pests take one sip, kick up their heels and die.

They never find out what Hostathion is.
Triazophos remains the merest word,
Though partly echoed by the acrid fizz
Which suddenly grows too loud to be heard.

Hostathion was once Achilles' friend,
Staunch at his elbow before Ilios,
But now that name brings pea moth a quick end
Assisted by the cruel Triazophos.

Heroic words are too brave for the deeds
They do, yet maybe now they do less evil –
Ferocious but in service to our needs,
Venting our wrath for us on the seed weevil.

Forests of swords on the Homeric plain
Are momentarily invoked. Well, then,
It says much for this age where we complain
Men die like flies, that flies should die like men.

Triazophos sailed with Hostathion
Through centuries as if this were their goal:
Infinite enemies to fall upon,
Killing so common it is called control.

The prancing pudendum curls its lip but says Yes to Life:
It is a yea-neigher.
Not only does it say 'ha-ha!' among the trumpets,
But in the landscaped gardens of fashionable country houses
It trumpets among the ha-has,
And the pulsing vein of its back is not afraid.

Though fleet-footed as an Arab it is stronger than a Clydesdale,
Shouldered like a Shire, bulk-bodied like a Suffolk –
A standing, foam-flanked reproach
To all those of us more appropriately represented
By the Shetland pony,
Or that shrunken, shrivelled toy horse with the mule-tail
Equus przewalskii, Prejvalsky's horse
From the Kobdo district of western Mongolia.

At nightfall the women of storm-swept lonely farms,
Or at casement windows of the grand houses aforesaid,
Or women anywhere who languish unfulfilled *qua* women,
Feel their ontological divide transformed to jelly
At the vibrant snuffle in the distance –
Long to subdue it, to overcome it, to pacify it,
Willing it homeward to its chosen stable,
Which will suffer its presence all the more exquisitely
For being neither deep nor wide enough wholly to contain

The unbridled ambition of the philosophical phallus.

Egon Friedell's Heroic Death

Egon Friedell committed suicide
By jumping from his window when he saw
Approaching Brownshirts eager to preside
At rites the recent *Anschluss* had made law.

Vienna's coffee-house habitués
By that time were in Paris, Amsterdam,
London, New York. Friedell just couldn't raise
The energy to take it on the lam.

Leaving aside the question of their looks,
The Jews the Nazis liked to see in Hell
Were good at writing and owned lots of books –
Which all spelled certain curtains for Friedell.

Friedell was cultivated in a way
That now in Europe we don't often see.
For every volume he'd have had to pay
In pain what those thugs thought the fitting fee.

Forestalling them was simply common sense,
An act only a Pharisee would blame,
Yet hard to do when fear is so intense.
Would *you* have had the nerve to do the same?

The normal move would be to just lie still
And tell yourself you somehow might survive,
But this great man of letters had the will
To meet his death while he was still alive.

So out into the air above the street
He sailed with all his learning left behind,
And by one further gesture turned defeat
Into a triumph for the human mind.

The civilised are most so as they die.
He called a warning even as he fell
In case his body hit a passer-by
As innocent as was Egon Friedell.

Homage to Rafinesque

The ichthyologist Constantine Rafinesque-Schmaltz
(Who was pleased to be known as quite simply Rafinesque)
And John James Audubon the famous student of birds
(Whose folios are generally thought too gorgeous for words
Although when opened they envelop your entire desk)
Teamed up in America as if they were dancing a waltz.

It was neither fish nor fowl crabbed their double act.
The flap in their cabin was caused by a humble bat
Which Rafinesque with the nearest thing to hand attacked,
Thus pounding Audubon's beloved violin out flat.

The revenge Audubon took was oblique but sure.
He returned from the Ohio River with drawings, life-size,
Of fish Rafinesque hadn't seen hide nor hair of before,
But belief in Audubon's pencil put scales on his eyes.

He published a book which his enemies loved for its faults.
To pay with his fame for a fiddle was clearly grotesque.
With the object of leading his friend up a similar creek
He might justly have fashioned a phoenix claw or orc beak,
But he showed the forbearance implied by his name,
    Rafinesque.
Now Audubon's plates are hoarded like gold in the vaults

And only the fish honour Constantine Rafinesque-Schmaltz.

Will Those Responsible Come Forward?

May the Lord have mercy on all those peoples
Who suffer from a perversion of religion –
Or, to put it in a less equivocating way,
Who suffer from an excess of religion –
Or, to come right out with it,
Who suffer from religion.

Let Him tell those catholic protestants or protestant catholics
Who in Northern Ireland go to bed on Saturday night
Looking forward to a morning of Holy Worship
That just this once they should make other plans –
Have a heavy cold, a stomach upset or a pulled hamstring
Severe enough to render them immobile,
With something similar for their children –
So that they will not be there to form a congregation
In a church just big enough for a small massacre.
Arrange this reprieve, Lord,
And if you can't manage that much then for Christ's sake
Hand the whole deal over to Allah.

May the Lord with the assistance of Allah
Give heed to the cries of those children in Beirut
Who have the dubious luck to be ten years old and under
While dwelling in the vicinity of a PLO faction
Currently being wiped out by another PLO faction,
And kindly swing it so that the incoming rockets
Do not dismember their small persons irreparably.
Children older than ten years we will give up on,
Not wanting the moon,
And their mothers, needless to say, are for the high jump.
Fix it, Lord. Get Al on to it,
And if it turns out to be more than you can handle
Raise Jehovah on the horn.

May the Lord and Allah with Jehovah's proverbial
In-depth back-up and sales apparatus
Make a concerted effort to cut the crap,
For the following reasons among others:

Lest at least two kinds of Christians during their annual shoot-
  out
Bisect an old lady who hears the word 'Duck!'
But can't hit the deck because of sciatica
(May her stoop be steep) –

Lest the Druze and the Jews or the Juze and the Drews,
When shelling each other from somewhere each side
Of a ridge or a bridge,
Cascade hot shrapnel on the intervening hospital
Whose patients suffer from mental disorders,
And thus exacerbate in those unstable minds
An already acute sense of insecurity
(May their strait-jackets be flak-jackets) –

Lest Iraq and Iran or Iran and Iraq go to rack and ruin
Not just in the standard Islamic manner
Of finding each other insufficiently fanatical,
But with an ironic new wrinkle
By which the hitherto unapproachably sordid
Ayatollah or Arsola
Is upstaged by his own appointee,
That even more sadistic fuckwit and fruitcake
The Hayula or Payola,
Who has women tortured in front of their husbands
As a forceful reminder, no doubt supererogatory,
That you can't fight central mosque
(May their screams be deafening) –

Who also, if that doesn't do the trick,
Has the children tortured along with their mothers
(May they all go crazy quickly),
The object being to make the fathers admit
That they plotted the regime's overthrow –
A pretty fantastic charge when you consider
That the regime's overthrow hasn't yet been accomplished
By Allah functioning either on his tod
Or in combination with the Lord, Jehovah,
Buddha, the Great Spirit and each and every other
Recognised form of God –

Always supposing that They are working on it.
Always supposing that They care
About that or anything else.

But this is the sin of despair.

Echo Echo Echo

Changes in temperature entail turmoil.
Petits pois palpitate before they boil.
Ponds on the point of freezing look like oil
And God knows what goes on below the soil.

God and the naturalists, who penetrate
With camera crews to depths as dark as fate
And shoot scenes hideous to contemplate
Where burrowing Attenboroughs fight and mate.

In outer space the endless turbulence
Seems too far gone to be at our expense.
One likes to think that if a bang's immense
It didn't happen in the present tense.

Still it's unnerving when two galaxies –
One Catherine wheel and one like a Swiss cheese –
Get stuck in with sharp elbows and scraped knees,
Cancelling out their twin eternities.

As for inside the atom here at home,
It makes the cosmos look like *jeu de paume*
Played out around the Houston Astrodome.
We might as well be back in ancient Rome.

Random, unjust and violent universe!
We feel, and those less ignorant feel worse,
Knowing that what's observed must soon disperse
And Phaethon's car turn out to be a hearse.

Hence, or despite that, our concern with form,
Though even here outclassed by nature's norm.
Snowflakes knock spots off Philibert de L'Orme
But something tells us that they are not warm.

Not that *we* are, compared with, say, the worms
Who live on lava, or are those the germs
That breed in butane and eat isotherms?
I'm not much good with scientific terms.

Even for Einstein it remained a dream
To unify the field, which makes it seem
Likely the rest of us won't get a gleam
Of how, or if, the whole works fit a scheme.

One merely hopes that we have made a start.
Our apprehensions might not melt the heart
Or even be heartfelt for the most part,
But from that insufficiency comes art.

We gather ourselves up from the abyss
As lovers after copulation kiss –
Lip-service which, while semaphoring bliss,
Puts in a claim that there was point to this.

Small wonder, therefore, that from time to time,
As dollar millionaires still nickel-and-dime,
The free-form poet knuckles down to rhyme –
Scared into neatness by the wild sublime.

The Anchor of the *Sirius*

Triangular Macquarie Place, up from the Quay,
Is half rain forest, half a sculpture park
Where can be found – hemmed in by palms and ferns,
Trees touching overhead – the Obelisk
From which, one learns, All Public Roads are Measured
Leading to the Interior of the Colony.
Skyscraper cliffs keep this green garden dark.

The Obelisk is sandstone. Thomas Mort
Is also present, bronze on a tall plinth –
His plain Victorian three-piece suit bulks large,
Befitting Sydney's first successful exporter
Of refrigerated foods – while, lower down
This plush declivity, one finds a bubbler
Superfluously shaded by a small
But intricate gun-metal *baldacchino*,
Sure-footed as a Donatello font.

Thus in a sculpture court less up to date
Yet cooler than MOMA's, leafier than the Frick,
One strolls encountering pieces carried out
In traditional materials and is lulled –
Till this free-standing object looms and startles
Like a Calder by Duchamp. It stops you cold,
The anchor of the *Sirius*. It hooks you
More firmly than the fluke which can't be seen
(Because, presumably, buried in the earth)
Could ever have snared the bottom of Sydney Cove.

One is amazed by how it is not old –
Which means the Colony's protracted birth
(The women were outscreamed by the flayed men)
Falls so far short of being long ago
It's hard to grasp. The anchor was brought back
From where the ship ended its history –
I think it tried to sail through Norfolk Island –.

[26]

To where it began ours. Yes, the First Fleet
Dropped its first anchor just one hundred yards
(Or metres, as they say now) down the street –
And this is it, not much more touched by time
Than now by me, a yokel in the museum.

The crops failed. Phillip was no dynamo,
But Macquarie was, and men like Mort could double
The town's wealth in ten years. The scrub grew long
And lush like Joan Sutherland's throat. Success
Went overseas, took umpteen curtain calls,
Was toasted and had toast named after it,
And now the audience is here. Out on the harbour
Captain Cook II jam-packed with Japanese,
Their Nikons crackling like automatic flak,
Goes swanning past the well-remembered line
Where the submarine nets were when I was young,
Forty years ago – i.e. a full
Fifth of the time Port Jackson's had that name.

And after I'd grown up and gone away
Like the wool-clip to the other end of the world
(Where the wool was turned to suit-cloth and sent back
So Thomas Mort, full of ideas as Dickens,
Might look the part of the philanthropist)
The anchor of the *Sirius* had me pinned –
Spiked, rooted to the spot under these trees
Which filter what light's left by the glass towers
They put up yesterday so that the banks –
Algemene Bank Nederland NV,
Dresdner Bank AG, Banco Nazionale del Lavoro,
Sumitomo International Finance Australia –
Might catch through tinted windows like hot news
Digits conveying all they need to know,
Drawn down from space by ranks of VDUs
And here made manifest as a green glow –
New York and London, Hong Kong, Tokyo,
Sucked in at once to this same lightning rod –
Completing their great journey from afar
As a tired sinner comes at last to God,
As a ship comes in and drops anchor.

The Ferry Token

Not gold but some base alloy, it stays good
For one trip though the currency inflates –
Hard like the ferry's deck of seasoned wood,
The only coin in town that never dates.

Don Juan, as described by Baudelaire,
Before he crossed the Styx to the grim side
Paid Charon *son obole*, his ferry fare.
Was it this very token, worth one ride?

Of course it wasn't. This poor thing will buy
The traveller no myth beyond the dark
Leonine Pinchgut with one beady eye
Fixed on the brilliant, beckoning Luna Park.

At most it takes you back to Billy Blue
Whose ferry linked the Quay to the North Shore
Somewhere about the year of Waterloo –
And probably more after than before.

There's been so little time for grand events.
One ferry sank, but saying those who drowned
Contributed to our historic sense
Would be obscene and logically unsound.

Nevertheless nostalgia impregnates
This weightless disc as sunlight bleaches wood.
Our past is shallow but it scintillates –
Not gold but some base alloy, it stays good.

Funnelweb

The flame reflected in the welder's mask
Burns the board-rider's upstage fingertips
That cut a swathe across the curved sea-wall
Inside the Banzai Pipeline's tubular swell.
Sopranos feel the same fire on their lips
Kissing Jochanaan as befits the task.

The crank-winged Chance-Vought F4-U Corsair
When turning tightly spilled white vortices
Behind its wing-tips in the cobalt blue.
A mere machine, a Running W
As once brought stuntmen's horses to their knees,
And yet you can't deny it carved the air.

Phenomena like these, it will be said,
Are only incidental at the most
And mostly trivial, to say the least:
Less the confetti at the wedding feast
Than the box it came in, spice without the roast,
Beaches at Tarawa without the dead.

A saturation diver sets his seal
Where even fish can't see reflected flame.
A surfer in the folded tube may form
His signature unnoticed from the foam.
Night fighters' ailerons worked just the same
And Salome might think of her next meal.

True, but not true enough, in my belief.
These things though tenuous aren't set apart.
The casual grace-note can't help but imply,
If not the outline of the melody,
Then anyway the impulse at its heart –
And do so all the more for being brief.

Stillness in movement is a waking dream
Movement in stillness has refined from strength.
The river bank must make the drift apparent
Of swans at evening plugged into the current,
But lest they be disorganised at length
Just out of sight they steer to point upstream.

Wristy Makarova's Odette/Odile
(Two lovely people spinning on one toe)
Exemplifies the Body Beautiful
Consumed by its own power to appal.
Watch how the whiplash whirlwind sucks up snow –
A double helix drawn from sex appeal.

Woodcut adoring kings with narrowed eye
Quite clearly find the cradle-capped young Prince
Painful to look at, backed up by his nimbus.
Even His Mother, pierced by the columbus
And haloed in Her own right, seems to wince:
The sun is in the wrong part of the sky.

He could not save Himself, they said with scorn,
But always it has been supposed they erred
And that, armed by His power to distinguish
The star-bursts in His hands from human anguish,
He ultimately went out like a bird
The way that He came in when He was born.

Watching a dear friend go down fast with cancer
Like a raindrop down a window pane, I hold
Her hand of balsa clad with clear doped silk
Pulsating like the skin of simmering milk
Which must boil over soon and leave her cold.
Next time *I'm* coming back a necromancer.

The floorboards in Kyoto's Nijo-jo
Will sing like flocks of birds from their sleeved nails
When someone walks, however light in weight.
Thus Tokugawa shoguns dreamed at night
Equating sudden death with nightingales,
And paper walls seemed real, this being so.

Saito himself committed suicide
The long way round by using the short sword
Before the banzai charge went in at dawn.
Three thousand died before the sun went down.
All night it sounded like a psycho ward.
We sacked out with the corpses open-eyed.

What happened the next morning broke your heart.
We saw the whole thing from above the beach.
Mothers threw living babies from the cliff.
The sick lined up to have their heads hacked off.
Those soldiers that the non-coms couldn't reach
Kissed a grenade and blew themselves apart.

Marines you'd swear would never shed a tear
On Saipan wept. And that was all she wrote.
We just got used to it, like swatting flies.
Not even Iwo came as a surprise.
The whole Jap nation would have cut its throat
I swear to God sure as I'm standing here.

For Lichtenberg, wit was a microscope,
Yet in between the lines he seemed to know
His fine analysis did not disperse,
But gave coherence to, the universe.
That strong light touch sums up the rococo:
An epoch blown from clear glass, not from soap.

So do the buildings of Cuvilliés,
The Wittelsbachs' great court-dwarf architect,
Whose play of curlicue and arabesque
Like flame reflected in the welder's mask
Suggests a brilliance beyond intellect,
Fulfilled creation singing its own praise.

His small theatre of the Residenz
In World War II was bombed to smithereens
Yet could be put back as it was, because
Its dazzling inner shell was lath and gauze,
A kit of plaster panels and silk screens
They stashed away until the world saw sense.

At Vegas, the last Grand Prix of the year
Before he died in Belgium, Gilles Villeneuve
Put on his helmet and I saw the sun
Fill up his tinted visor like white wine.
Few poets get the face that they deserve
Or, like Hart Crane, can travel in a tear.

Of course Villeneuve was handsome anyway –
The Rimbaud of the wheel just oozed romance –
But where his class showed was in how that beast
Ferrari drew sweet curves at his behest
Instead of leading him St Vitus' dance.
He charged the earth but gave back art for pay.

If she could *see* herself, the girl on skates –
But she must work by feel in the event,
Assured by how her heavy fingers burn
As in mid-air she makes the triple turn
Explosive effort was correctly spent
And from the whirlpool a way out awaits.

They say that Pipeline surfers deep in white
Whipped water when wiped out may sip the froth
Through pursed lips and thus drown less than they breathe
While buffeted their helpless bodies writhe,
Then once the ruined wave has spent its wrath
Swim resurrected up to the bright light.

Though children in deep shelters could not watch,
Pathfinder flares were sumptuous where they burned
And rustic simpletons found food for thought
In how those coloured chandeliers would float
As if the Son of Man had just returned –
Before the earthquake made them a hotch-potch.

Descending from heaped rubble, 'I composed
Der Rosenkavalier,' Strauss told GIs
Whose billet underneath the *Führerbau*
Reminded them of their hometown hoosegow.
At eighty he was right, if scarcely wise:
From where he stood the episode was closed.

And soon there was another Salome
To propagate his long *legato* phrases,
And, by their shapeliness made feverish,
Lift high the prophet's lopped head in a dish,
And taste the everlasting fire that rages
On those cold lips of *papier mâché.*

She's gone, perhaps to start again elsewhere.
The freezing fens lock up their latent heat.
The rime ice on the river to the touch
Splits in a gash benign neglect will stitch.
Full of potential like briquettes of peat
Atomic bombs enjoy conditioned air.

The Emperor's portrait had survived the blast.
We carried it to safety in the stream
And took turns holding it aloft. The fire
Arched overhead and we succumbed to fear.
The surface of the water turned to steam.
I must say we were very much downcast.

Emerging from a silo of spun spunk
To scan the killing-ground with clustered eyes,
The funnelweb when she appears in person
Reveals a personality pure poison
Should you be tempted to idealise
Her gauze-lined bunker under the tree trunk,

And yet how sweet a tunnel in the mist!
Well might it fascinate as well as frighten.
Looking along such lustrous holes in space
Where indrawn starlight corkscrews down the sluice,
You'll feel your heart first hammer and then lighten
And think God was a gynaecologist.

The Sun so far has only twice touched Earth
With its unmitigated baleful stare.
Flesh turned to pizza under that hot look.
From all the forms of death you took pot luck,
But that by which the occasion was made rare
Showed later on in what was brought to birth.

[33]

At KZ Dachau the birthmarked young nun
Beseeching absolution for that place
Won't turn her full face to your chapel pew.
Only her murmurs will admonish you
For thinking to give up pursuit of grace
Simply because such dreadful things were done.

High over Saipan when another plane
Came back above us heading for Japan
As we flew south for home, I never saw
What would have been a chromium gewgaw,
But only what it casually began –
A long straight line of crystal flake cocaine.

Your progeny won't sit still to be told
Nor can you point out through the window how
Air battles of the past left vapour trails
Swirling and drifting like discarded veils,
Scarcely there then and not at all there now,
Except you feel the loss as you grow old.

Black-bottomed whiteware out of nowhere fast
The Shuttle takes fire coming back to us,
A purple storm with silence at the core.
Simmering down, it is the dodgem car
Daedalus should have given Icarus,
Whose wings – a bad mistake – were built to last.

To stay the course you must have stuff to burn.
For life, the ablative is absolute,
And though the fire proceeds against our wishes
Forms are implicit even in the ashes
Where we must walk in an asbestos suit:
A smouldering tip to which all things return.

We may not cavalierly lift the casque
Which separates us from the consequences
Of seeing how the godhead in full bloom
Absolves itself unthinkingly from blame.
It knows us as we know it, through our senses.
We feel for it the warmth in which we bask –

The flame reflected in the welder's mask.

[34]

A Valediction for Philip Larkin

You never travelled much but now you have,
Into the land whose brochures you liked least:
That drear Bulgaria beyond the grave
Where wonders have definitively ceased –
Ranked as a dead loss even in the East.

Friends will remember until their turn comes
What they were doing when the news came through.
I landed in Nairobi with eardrums
Cracked by the flight from Kichwa Tembo. You
Had gone, I soon learned, on safari too.

Learned soon but too late, since no telephone
Yet rings in the wild country where we'd been.
No media penetration. On one's own
One wakes up and unzips the morning scene
Outside one's tent and always finds it green.

Green Hills of Africa, wrote Hemingway.
Omitting a preliminary 'the',
He made the phrase more difficult to say –
The hills, however, easier to see,
Their verdure specified initially.

Fifty years on, the place still packs a thrill.
Several reserves of greenery survive,
And now mankind may look but must not kill
Some animals might even stay alive,
Surrounded by attentive four-wheel-drive

Toyotas full of tourists who shoot rolls
Of colour film off in the cheetah's face
While she sleeps in the grass or gravely strolls
With bloody cheeks back from the breathless chase,
Alone except for half the human race.

But we patrolled a less well-beaten trail.
Making a movie, we possessed the clout
To shove off up green hill and down green dale
And put our personal safety in some doubt
By opening the door and getting out.

Thus I descended on the day you died
And had myself filmed failing to get killed.
A large male lion left me petrified
But well alone and foolishly fulfilled,
Feeling weak-kneed but calling it strong-willed.

Silk brushed with honey in the hot noon light,
His inside leg was colonised by flies.
I made a mental note though wet with fright.
As his mouth might have done off me, my eyes
Tore pieces off him to metabolise.

In point of fact I swallowed Kenya whole,
A mill choked by a plenitude of grist.
Like anabolic steroids for the soul,
Every reagent was a catalyst –
So much to take in sent me round the twist.

I saw Kilimanjaro like the wall
Of Heaven going straight up for three miles.
The Mara river was a music hall
With tickled hippos rolling in the aisles.
I threw some fast food to the crocodiles.

I chased giraffes who floated out of reach
Like anglepoise lamps loose in zero g.
I chased a *mdudu* with a can of bleach
Around my tent until I couldn't see.
Only a small rhinoceros chased me.

The spectral sun-bird drew the mountain near,
And if the rain-bird singing *soon soon soon*
Turned white clouds purple, still the air was clear –
The radiant behind of a baboon
Was not more opulent than the full moon.

So one more tourist should have been agog
At treasure picked up cheaply while away –
Ecstatic as some latterday sea-dog,
His trolley piled high like a wain of hay
With duty-free goods looted from Calais.

For had I not enlarged my visual scope,
Perhaps my whole imaginative range,
By seeing how that dead-pan antelope,
The topi, stands on small hills looking strange
While waiting for the traffic lights to change?

And had I not observed the elephant
Deposit heaps of steaming excrement
While looking wiser than Immanuel Kant,
More stately than the present Duke of Kent?
You start to see why I was glad I went.

Such sights were trophies, ivory and horn
Destined for carving into *objets d'art*.
Ideas already jumping like popcorn,
I climbed down but had not gone very far
Between that old Dakota and the car

When what they told me stretched the uncrossed space
Into a universe. No tears were shed.
Forgive me, but I hardly felt a trace
Of grief. Just sudden fear your being dead
So soon had left us disinherited.

You were the one who gave us the green light
To get out there and seek experience,
Since who could equal you at sitting tight
Until the house around you grew immense?
Your bleak bifocal gaze was so intense,

Hull stood for England, England for the world –
The whole caboodle crammed into one room.
Above your desk all of creation swirled
For you to look through with increasing gloom,
Or so your poems led us to assume.

[37]

Yet even with your last great work 'Aubade'
(To see death clearly, did you pull it close?)
The commentator must be on his guard
Lest he should overlook the virtuose
Technique which makes majestic the morose.

The truth is that you revelled in your craft.
Profound glee charged your sentences with wit.
You beat them into stanza form and laughed:
They didn't sound like poetry one bit,
Except for being absolutely it.

Described in English written at its best
The worst of life remains a bitch to face
But is more shared, which leaves us less depressed –
Pleased the condition of the human race,
However desperate, is touched with grace.

The seeming paradox is a plain fact –
You brought us all together on your own.
Your saddest lyric is a social act.
A bedside manner in your graveyard tone
Suggests that at the last we aren't alone.

You wouldn't have agreed, of course. You said
Without equivocation that life ends
With him who lived it definitely dead
And buried, after which event he tends
To spend a good deal less time with his friends.

But you aren't here to argue. Where you are
By now is anybody's guess but yours.
I'm five miles over Crete in a Tristar
Surrounded by the orchestrated snores
Induced by some old film of Roger Moore's.

Things will be tougher now you've proved your point
By leaving early, that the man upstairs
Neither controls what happens in the joint
We call the world, nor noticeably cares.
While being careful not to put on airs,

It is perhaps the right time to concede
That life is all downhill from here on in.
For doing justice to it, one will need,
If not in the strict sense a sense of sin,
More *gravitas* than fits into a grin.

But simply staying put makes no one you.
Those who can't see the world in just one street
Must see the world. What else is there to do
Except face inescapable defeat
Flat out in a first-class reclining seat?

You heard the reaper in the Brynmor Jones
Library cough behind your swivel chair.
I had to hear those crocodiles crunch bones,
Like cars compressed for scrap, before the hair
Left on my head stood straight up in the air.

You saw it all in little. You dug deep.
A lesser man needs coarser stimuli,
Needs coruscating surfaces . . . needs sleep.
I'm very rarely conscious when I fly.
Not an event in life. To sleep. To die.

I wrote that much, then conked out over Rome,
Dreamed I'd been sat on by a buffalo,
Woke choking as we tilted down for home,
And now see, for once cloudless, the pale glow
Of evening on the England you loved so

And spoke for in a way she won't forget.
The quiet voice whose resonance seemed vast
Even while you lived, and which has now been set
Free by the mouth that shaped it shutting fast,
Stays with us as you turn back to the past –

Your immortality complete at last.

Parodies, Imitations
and Lampoons

From Robert Lowell's Notebook

Notes for a Sonnet

Stalled before my metal shaving mirror
With a locked razor in my hand I think of Tantalus
Whose lake retreats below the fractured lower lip
Of my will. Splinter the groined eyeballs of our sin,
Ford Madox Ford: you on the Quaker golf-course
In Nantucket double-dealt your practised lies
Flattering the others and me we'd be great poets.
How wrong you were in their case. And now Nixon,
Nixon rolls in the harpoon ropes and smashes with his flukes
The frail gunwales of our beleaguered art. What
Else remains now but your England, Ford? There's not
Much Lowell-praise left in Mailer but could be Alvarez
Might still write that book. In the skunk-hour
My mind's not right. But there will be
Fifty-six new sonnets by tomorrow night.

Revised Notes for a Sonnet

On the steps of the Pentagon I tucked my skull
Well down between my knees, thinking of Cordell Hull
Cabot Lodge Van du Plessis Stuyvesant, our gardener,
Who'd stop me playing speedway in the red-and-rust
Model A Ford that got clapped out on Cape Cod
And wound up as a seed-shed. Oh my God, my God,
How this administration bleeds but will not die,
Hacking at the rib-cage of our art. You were wrong, R.P.
Blackmur. Some of the others had our insight, too:
Though I suppose I had endurance, toughness, faith,
Sensitivity, intelligence and talent. My mind's not right.
With groined, sinning eyeballs I write sonnets until dawn
Is published over London like a row of books by Faber –
Then shave myself with Uncle's full-dress sabre.

[43]

Notes for a Revised Sonnet

Slicing my head off shaving I think of Charles I
Bowing to the groined eyeball of Cromwell's sinning will.
Think too of Orpheus, whose disembodied head
Dumped by the Bacchants floated singing in the river,
His love for Eurydice surviving her dumb move
By many sonnets. Decapitation wouldn't slow me down
By more than a hundred lines a day. R.P. and F.M.F.
Play eighteen holes together in my troubled mind,
Ford faking his card, Blackmur explicating his,
And what is love? John Berryman, if you'd had what it took
We could have both blown England open. Now, alone,
With a plush new set-up to move into and shake down,
I snow-job Stephen Spender while the liquor flows like lava
In the parlour of the Marchioness of Dufferin and Ava.

Once Smitten, Twice Smitten

Peter Porter as Enobarbus

There goes her barge without me. Did she spot
Me lurking in the reeds as she swept by?
Ra only knows. What gets her I've not got.
No ranks below Triumvir need apply.

I'm just a scribe in plastic sandals. She
Squats on a golden throne, I on this log.
How does it feel to screw a dynasty?
Caesar found out, but he was not a wog.

And now it's Antony that fuels her fires.
The lucky bastard lies in wait down-Nile.
Some Keystone Copts are shouting. It transpires
I'm sitting on a sacred crocodile.

Adrian Henri Wants to Write Poems

Remembering the day I walked five miles in my short trousers
To draw a picture of a plover's nest
And found out when I got there
That my pencil was broken and I had nothing to sharpen it with
A Heinkel one-eleven flew overhead looking for Liverpool
Or was it a Zeppelin, it's hard to remember how old
you are when you've been working on a youth image this long
cranes in the dockyards foghorns on the water clouds in the sky
lying on my back in grandad's allotment discovering Mallarmé
seeing the world for the first time flowers earth grass weeds.
a sad young poet needing something to bring the brilliance of
    his perceptions
into focus

EUNICE tall dark schoolgirl breasts like fairy-cakes you show
    me
yours running up the sand hills sudden flash of knickers
    illuminating
a young poet's mind and showing him his future
SHARON small fair schoolgirl transforming herself at night into
    a ponytail teenager pressed up against me dancing to Guy
    Mitchell
breast knickers breast knickers knickers
SHARON'S MOTHER love-starved scolding horror screaming at
the sad young poet saying what have you done to my Sharon
    playing
hospitals realising with a shock that Sharon's mother wears
knickers
too

on a bus to London
reading Leopardi in the Heath-Stubbs translation
getting off at Victoria with an air-force hold-all
full of spare cuddle-pie pea-jackets, horn-rimmed glasses
and four thousand seven hundred pages of single-spaced
    manuscript
Pete Brown running towards me inspired liberated cute
yelling hey Adrian the whole poetry-reading circuit is opening
    up the way Eunice used to and me yelling back
watch out for that bus
too late
in the Royal Free hospital Pete with all four limbs in traction
a splint up his nose and his mouth wired together
and the sad young poet sitting beside his bed
reads the whole manuscript Pete signalling gratitude
with his left eyebrow

Edinburgh Festival lights fame repression
streets full of scotsmen Royal Mile chips haggis
Traverse theatre lunchtimes reading with Roger McGough
girls packed along the walls drinking in every word
knickers knickers knickers knickers

then you happened
middle-aged woman with body of a schoolgirl
lying all night on top of you like Moby Dick in dry dock
reciting Mallarmé to the rhythm of your loving
saying are you really twenty years old and hearing you sob
no thirty-four

then she happened
girl beautiful as cup-cakes frilly-edged knickers
lying all night on top of her reciting Leopardi
saying are you really twenty years old and hearing her sob
no eleven

In Wormwood scrubs the sad young poet reads Rimbaud in the
    library
working on the autobiography Cape yelling for more
    instalments
dreaming of schoolgirls in cell at night
warm young bodies under blue gym slips open mouths questing
    hands
rain slanting down past the barred window
Brown making a million writing lyrics for Cream
got to get out of here, back in amongst it
fame knickers wealth adulation wealth knickers fame knickers
knickers
sad young poet writing on into the night

R. S. Thomas at Altitude

The reason I am leaning over
At this pronounced angle is simply
That I am accustomed to standing
On Welsh hillsides
Staring out over escarpments stripped
And pitiless as my vision,
Where God says: Come
Back to the trodden manure
Of the chapel's warm temptation.
But I see the canker that awaits
The child, and say no.
I see the death that ends
Life, and say no.
Missing nothing, I say
No, no.
And God says: you can't
Say no to me, cully,
I'm omnipotent.
But I indicate the
Flying birds and the
Swimming fish and the trudging
Horse with my pointing
Finger and with customary
Economy of language, say
Nothing.
There is a stone in my mouth,
There is a storm in my
Flesh, there is a wind in
My bone.
Artificer of the knuckled, globed years
Is this your answer?
I've been up on this hill
Too long.

Edward Estlin Cummings Dead

what time el Rouble & la Dollar spin
'their' armies into ever smaller change,
patrolling Kopeks for a Quarter search
& Deutschfranc, after decimating Yen
inflates with sterling Rupee in a ditch

(what time, i.e., as moneys in their 'death'
throes leave room for unbought souls to breathe)

that time, perhaps,
                        I'm him believing (i.
e., cummings
   hold it
   CUMMINGS) dead (

p   e   g   g   e   d   o   u   t
) & I will leave him lie

John Wain's Letters to Five More Artists

I

Now that I am Oxford Professor of Poetry, Django Reinhardt,
I salute your memory with more humility than ever.
You with crippled hands
Plucked everlasting beauty on that Dicky Wells
Paris Concert LP that I wore out.
You thought that different moons shone over France and
    England
But you played something superlative every time. No
    intellectual,
You were all artist. I wish, increasingly, that I were less
Intellectual. I would like to be a gipsy guitarist
With his fingers burned off playing with Dicky Wells,
Matching glittering silver guitar-runs to the black ripeness
Of his golden horn. I find, myself,
That to be prolific comes easily
But to be memorable takes effort. I wish
I could do what you did on *La Mer*. Wish also, Django, *mon
    cher*,
That I could be more humble.

II

Now that I am Oxford Professor of Poetry, Michelangelo
    Buonarotti,
I revere your achievement and feel increasingly less complacent.
The culture which gave rise to you had everything you needed
Except the Wolfenden Report. You could design buildings,
Write sonnets in Italian, and when you painted a ceiling
It stayed painted. But above all, you could sculpt.
Michelangelo, *amico*, you once said

[51]

That you chipped away the marble until you found the statue
  inside.
As a poet I have been using the same technique for years, and
  wish
That I could be even less complacent than I am now. *Capito*?

P.S. Could you use a few bags of marble chips? I've
Got a garage full.

III

Now that I am Oxford Professor of Poetry, Wolfgang Amadeus
  Mozart,
The mere mention of your name brings me up short, wishing
That I had made better use of my time. At my age
You had been dead for years, yet look
At the stuff you turned out. *Figaro. Don Giovanni.* K488.
The Flute.
You never finished your Requiem, of course; and I try to take
Comfort from that. As a business brain, you were a non-starter
And freemasonry was a blind alley. You would never have
  made it
To the Oxford Chair of Poetry. But taken as a whole
Yours was a career that leaves a modern artist chastened.
My poem *Wildtrack* was influenced by the slow movement of
  your Fourth
Violin Concerto, although comparisons are odious. I bow.
Schlaf' wohl, Wolfgang – precursor of us all.

IV

Now that I am Oxford Professor of Poetry, Rainer Maria Rilke,
I think of your prodigious gift and quell my surge of pride.
What was it, three-quarters of the *Duinos* and all the *Sonnets
To Orpheus* written in two weeks? Not even *Wildtrack*
Came as such a protean outpouring. And you had connections,
   Bruder:
Contacts dwarfing anything of ours. Weekends
In cloud-scraping Bavarian *Schlosses* with aristocratic women!
*Aus dem besitz der Grafin-Königen Marie von Thurn-und-
   Taxis Hohenlohe*
You inscribed, while my lot dedicated stuff to Sadie Bloggs.
You make me feel small, Rainer, *mein Freund, Dichter.*
As do Wolfgang, Mike and Django.

V

Now that I am Oxford Professor of Poetry, Stephen Spender,
I would just like to say Tough Luck, Baby
But that's the way the cookie crumbles. Someone has to lose,
So eat my dust.
The thirties haven't got it in the nuts any more. My turn,
   padrone.
But stick around. We haven't forgotten how you old guys
Opened up the rackets for the new ideas. Times have changed,
But we'll find some action that fits your style. Can you drive?

Symptoms of Self-Regard

As she lies there naked on the only hot
Day in a ruined August reading Hugo Williams,
She looks up at the window-cleaner
Who has hesitantly appeared.

Wishing that he were Hugo Williams
She luxuriates provocatively,
Her fantasy protected by the glass
Or so she thinks.

Would that this abrasive oaf
Were Hugo Williams, she muses –
Imagining the poet in a black Armani
Bomber jacket from *Miami Vice*,
His lips pursed to kiss.

Suddenly, convulsively, she draws
The sheet up over herself
And quivers, having at last realised
That it really *is* Hugo Williams.

He sinks out of sight,
His poem already written.
He signs it 'Hugo Williams'.
The blue overalls have come in handy.

He takes off his flat cap,
Letting his silken hair fall free.
Hugo Williams has gone back to being handsome.
The poet has come down to earth.

Richard Wilbur's Fabergé Egg Factory

If Occam's Razor gleams in Massachusetts
In time the Pitti Palace is unravelled:
An old moon re-arising as the new sets
To show the poet how much he has travelled.

Laforgue said missing trains was beautiful
But Wittgenstein said words should not seduce:
Small talk from him would at the best be dutiful –
And news of trains, from either man, no use.

Akhmatova finds echoes in Akhnaten.
The vocables they share *a fortiori*
Twin-yolk them in the self-same kindergarten
Though Alekhine might tell a different story.

All mentioned populate a limpid lyric
Where learning deftly intromits precision:
The shots are Parthian, the victories Pyrrhic,
Piccarda's ghost was not so pale a vision,

But still you must admit this boy's got class –
His riddles lead through vacuums to a space
Where skill leans on the parapet of farce
And sees Narcissus making up his face.

Godfrey in Paradise

Admirers of Godfrey Smith's Sunday Times *column, one of whose principal concerns is the various promotional free meals to which he is invited, were not surprised to learn, from a recent feature article by him in the same newspaper, that lunch is his idea of heaven.*

When Godfrey Smith goes up to Heaven
He'll see more cream teas than in Devon
And angels in McDonald's hats
Ladling chips from golden vats.

Because he has been very good
Godfrey will smell all kinds of grub:
Lancashire hotpot, Yorkshire pud,
Saddle of lamb and syllabub.

When Godfrey breasts the pearly gates
Fat cherubs will bang spoons on plates,
Filling the air with chubby singing.
The gong for dinner will be ringing.

But dinner, Godfrey will intuit,
Leads on to breakfast, thence to brunch.
In Heaven there's no limit to it.
The whole thing's one enormous lunch.

Brie, Stilton, Roquefort and Caerphilly,
Banana splits *avec* Chantilly,
Petits fours, wafers, halvah, toffee
Come with, if not before, the coffee.

The scoff in Heaven's done just right.
The chocolate sauce is not too thick.
They do not beat the mousse all night
Nor oversteam the spotted dick.

When Godfrey dines with his Creator
He'll bung five quid to the head waiter
And compliment his beaming host
On the aroma of the roast.

The Koran promises its readers
Heaven's one endless copulation.
Godfrey will pity the poor bleeders
From his eternity of gustation.

What proper man would plump for bints
Ahead of After Eight thin mints?
True pleasure for a man of parts
Is tarts in him, not him in tarts.

When Godfrey Smith finds Paradise
He'll sniff that spread both long and broad
And start by eating it all twice –
The Lord's perpetual smorgasbord.

The Wasted Land

T. S. Tambiguiti

April is a very unkind month, I am telling you.
Oh yes. And summer was surprising us very much,
Coming over the Tottenham Court Road.
What are the roots that grab around you,
What are the branches that grow, actually,
Out of all this? Can't you tell me that?
You know only a heap of images all broken up.
Under the brown fog of a winter dawn,
A crowd was flowing over London Bridge, so many,
So many people there were crossing that bridge
It was looking like Calcutta.
There I was seeing somebody I knew and crying out
Rhanji! Rhanji! You who were with me
In that correspondence course they were giving
About how to repair railway engines
At home. Did you pass? But that was
A long time ago, oh yes, a long time ago.
Oh the moon shone very brightly on Mrs Murray
Who lived in Surrey.
She washed her feet in chicken curry.
Twit twit twit twit
Jug jug jug jug
Moo
It is unreal, this place, I am telling you that.
Do you listen to what I am telling you?
Burning burning burning burning burning
The whole vindaloo is burning, Ghita,
While you are talking to that silly Mrs Chatterjee.
These fragments I have shored against my ruins.
Hurry up please, you must be going home now.
Hurry up please, please hurry up.

Good night Rhanji. Good night Satyajit.
Good night Rabindranath. Good night Assistant
District Commissioner Cunningham-Price-Alyston.
Good night. Oh yes. It's good night that I am saying.
Good night. Good night. Tambiguiti is mad again.
Good night.
Shantih shantih shantih.
It's only a shantih in old
Shantih town.

After Such Knowledge

Great Tom: Notes Towards the Definition of T. S. Eliot by T. S. Matthews

I saw him when distaste had turned to nightmare
   Near the end of this interminable book:
   As if the terraced cloudscape were a staircase
And he himself yet palpable, his sandals,
   Achillean by asphodel uplifted,
   Propelled their burden's effortless ascent –
A tuft of candid feathers at each shoulder
   Proclaiming him apprentice, cherished fledgling
   To overhanging galleries of angels.
And so, the poet first and I behind him,
   But only he a freedman hieing homeward,
   My quarry turned towards me. I cried 'Master!
We all knew you could make it!' and embraced him –
   Since, being both Sordello and Odysseus,
   I forgot my teacher's substance was a shadow,
And gathered uselessly the empty air.
   'Just passing through?' he chuckled as I teetered,
   Perhaps to ease the anguish of my gesture.
'If I were you I wouldn't plan on staying,
   Unless you don't mind falling through the scenery.'
   His smile, admonitory yet seraphic,
Suggested Pentecost, the truce of Advent,
   The prior taste unspeakably assuaging
   Of the ineluctable apotheosis.
'You remember T. S. Matthews, Sir?' I asked.
   'T. S. Who?' 'He's written your biography.'
   'Matthews . . . I suppose I knew him vaguely.
A *Time* man. Is it awful?' A platoon
   Of cherubim flashed past us on the banister,
   Posteriors illumined by the marble:
The welcoming committee for Stravinsky,
   As yet some years below but toiling skyward.
   'Not quite as bad as most have said, but still
A pretty odious effort.' Here I wavered.
   Around his neck, the excalfactive Order
   Of Merit infumated, argentine,

But the gaze above, both placent and unsleeping,
   Entlastende without tergiversation,
   Compelled the apprehension it prevented.
And I: 'It hasn't got that many facts
   Which can't be found in places more reputed –
   Notably your widow's thoughtful preface
To the MS of *The Waste Land*. That aside,
   The speculative content can add little
   To the cairn of innuendo stacked already
By Sencourt's *T. S. Eliot: A Memoir*.'
   I paused. And he: 'Poor Robert was a pest,
   I'm sad to say. Well, all right: what's the fuss then?'
I caught a sudden flicker of impatience,
   Familiar yet ineffable. 'Sir, nothing;
   For nothing can come of nothing. Matthews puzzles
Repellently about those thousand letters
   You wrote to Emily Hale, but has no answers.'
   And he, diverted: 'Nor will anybody,
For another fifty years. I can't believe, though,
   A full-blown book enshrines no more than these
   Incursions void of judgment. Therefore speak.'
And I: 'He rates his chances as a critic –
   Allowing you your gift, he dares to offer
   Conjectures that your ear verged on the faulty.
You said, for instance, of St Magnus Martyr,
   Its walls contained inexplicable splendour.
   He calls that adjective cacophonous.'
'He calls it *what*?' 'Cacophonous.' 'I see.'
   And I: 'The strictures go beyond irreverence.
   His animus is manifest. Your consort
He terms "robust" at one point; elsewhere, "ample";
   Yet cravenly endorses in his foreword
   Her telling him in such a forthright manner
To render himself scarce.' A gust of laughter,
   Subversive of his sanctity, perturbed him.
   He conjured from the gold strings of his harp
An autoschediastic lilt of love
   Which might have once been whistled by Ravel.
   And he: 'She did that, did she? Excellent.'
I said, 'The pride you feel is not misplaced:

Your wish that no biography be written
  Will not be lightly flouted. Forced to yield,
Your wife will choose her author with great scruple
  Yet most of us who wish your memory well
  By now share the opinion that permission
To undertake the task must soon be granted
  Lest unofficial books like this gain ground,
  Besmirching the achievement of a lifetime.'
And he: 'I'm sure the lass will do what's best.
  One's not allowed to give advice from here
  And care for earthly fame is hard to summon.
It may, perhaps, however, please Another
  To whisper in her ear.' He turned away,
  Declaring as he faded 'It's surprising,
But this place isn't quite as Dante said –
  It's like the escalator at High Holborn,
  Except there's no way down.' So he departed,
Dissolving like a snowflake in the sun,
  A Sibyl's sentence in the leaves lost –
  Yet seemed like one who ends the race triumphant.

What About You? asks Kingsley Amis

When Mrs Taflan Gruffydd-Lewis left Dai's flat
She gave her coiffe a pat
Having straightened carefully those nylon seams
Adopted to fulfil Dai's wicked dreams.
Evans didn't like tights.
He liked plump white thighs pulsing under thin skirts in packed
    pubs on warm nights.

That's that, then, thought Evans, hearing her Jag start,
And test-flew a fart.
Stuffing the wives of these industrial shags may be all
Very well, and *this* one was an embassy bar-room brawl
With Madame Nhu.
Grade A. But give them that fatal twelfth inch and they'll soon
    take their cue

To grab a yard of your large intestine or include your glans
Penis in their plans
For that Rich, Full Emotional Life you'd thus far ducked
So successfully.
Yes, Evans was feeling . . . Mucked-
up sheets recalled their scrap.
Thinking barbed thoughts in stanza form after shafting's a right
    sweat. Time for a nap.

The North Window

To stay, as Mr Larkin stays, back late
Checking accessions in the Brynmor Jones
Library (the clapped date-stamp, punch-drunk, rattling,
The sea-green tinted windows turning slate,
The so-called Reading Room deserted) seems
A picnic at first blush. No Rolling Stones
Manqués or Pink Floyd simulacra battling
Their way to low-slung pass-marks head in hands:
Instead, unpeopled silence. Which demands

Reverence, and calls nightly like bad dreams
To make sure that that happens. Here he keeps
Elected frith, his thanedom undespited,
Ensconced against the mating-mandrill screams
Of this week's Students' Union Gang-Bang Sit-in,
As wet winds scour the Wolds. The moon-cold deeps
Are cod-thronged for the trawlers now benighted,
North. The inland cousin to the sail-maker
Can still bestride the boundaries of the way-acre,

The barley-ground and furzle-field unwritten
Fee simple failed to guard from Marks & Spencer's
Stock depot some time back. (Ten years, was it?)
Gull, lapwing, redshank, oyster-catcher, bittern
(Yet further out: sheerwater, fulmar, gannet)
Police his mud-and-cloud-ashlared defences.
Intangible revetments! On deposit,
Chalk thick below prevents the Humber seeping
Upward to where he could be sitting sleeping,

So motionless he lowers. Screwed, the planet
Swerves towards its distant, death-dark pocket.
He opens out his notebook at a would-be
Poem, ashamed by now that he began it.
Grave-skinned with grief, such Hardy-hyphened diction,
Tight-crammed as pack ice, grates. What keys unlock it?
It's all gone wrong. Fame isn't as it should be –
No, nothing like. 'The town's not been the same',
He's heard slags whine, 'since Mr Larkin came.'

Sir John arriving with those science-fiction
Broadcasting pricks and bitches didn't help.
And those Jap Ph.Ds, their questionnaires!
(Replying 'Sod off, Slant-Eyes' led to friction.)
He conjures envied livings less like dying:
Sharp cat-house stomp and tart-toned, gate-mouthed yelp
Of Satchmo surge undulled, dispersing cares
Thought reconvenes. In that way She would kiss,
The Wanted One. But other lives than this –

Fantastic. Pages spread their blankness. Sighing,
He knuckles down to force-feed epithets.
Would Love have eased the joints of his iambs?
He can't guess, and by now it's no use trying.
A sweet ache spreads from cramp-gripped pen to limb:
The stanza next to last coheres and sets.
As rhyme and rhythm, tame tonight like lambs,
Entice him to the standard whirlwind finish,
The only cry no distances diminish

Comes hurtling soundless from Creation's rim
Earthward – the harsh *recitativo secco*
Of spaces between stars. He hears it sing,
That voice of utmost emptiness. To him.
Declaring he has always moved too late,
And hinting, its each long-lost blaze's echo
Lack-lustre as a Hell-bent angel's wing,
That what – as if he needed telling twice –
Comes next makes this lot look like Paradise.

Verse Letters and Occasional Verse

To Russell Davies:
a letter from Cardiff

Dear Dai: I'm writing to you from location
For the new McKenzie film, in which I play
A role that would have filled me with elation
When I used to drink two-handed every day,
But as things are, it fills me with dismay –
With me no more than three weeks on the wagon
They're handing me free Foster's by the flagon.

I'm meant to be, you see, a drunken critic
Arrived in Europe from the Great South Land:
The least articulate, most paralytic
Plug-ugly in McKenzie's merry band,
Escorting that chaste hero on a grand
Excursion through the more arcane and zanier
Interstices of deepest Transylvania.

Which place we double here, in Cardiff (Wales),
Whose Burges follies neatly fill the bill:
They've even got the right-sized drawbridge nails.
Cold Castle Coch, perched darkly on a hill,
And Cardiff Castle in the city, will,
When cut together, serve as a spectacular
Surround for a larf riot spoofing Dracula.

Oh Cardiff! Dai, your homeland's sovereign seat,
This city of arcades and . . . more arcades,
I've hardly seen yet. Is there a main street?
No time for galleries or bookshop raids:
When precious shooting-time at evening fades
We shuttle back in vans to our hotel
And thank God that at least the beds work well

For nothing else there operates at all.
You risk your reason when you take your key.
They never wake you if you leave a call,
Do when you don't, refuse to give you tea
In bed unless asked not to – but get me.
I'm dining every evening in the presence
Of clown Dick Bentley, clever Donald Pleasence

And crazy Barry Humphries: no regrets.
On top of that, of course, I watch them work
Their wonders from sun-rise until it sets –
A feast of practised talent which I lurk
In awe to ogle, feeling like a berk.
I think, my friend, our highest common factor
The certainty we share that I'm no actor.

Whereas, of course, you are – about the best
I met at Cambridge. Have you given up
That gift to spend more effort on the rest?
Your dispositions overflow the cup.
No matter. Early days. The night's a pup.
Though there be times you'd like to see the back of
A few of all those trades you're such a Jack of

It's too soon to be certain what's dispensable.
You're bound to write more, draw more, play more jazz:
The man who brands your output reprehensible
You'll know to be a monomorph like Bazz,
Whose one-track mind's the only knack he has.
I fear our purist friends find nothing seedier
Than the way we spread ourselves around the Media,

But we both know you are, with all your bents,
As much compelled as I am with my few
To make from art and life some kind of sense
That leaves room for enjoying what we do.
Hermetic rhetoric aside, what's new
In serving more than one urge to excel
Like Michelangelo or Keith Michell?

Now I myself, though full-time a pop lyricist,
Have found the odd stint as a strict-form poet
Has rendered me less trusting, more empiricist,
Concerning technique and the need to know it.
This stuff you must make work or else you blow it.
Sincere intent alone is not enough:
For though the tone is light, the rules are tough.

The obstacle, says Gianfranco Contini,
Is what brings creativity to birth.
(His mind unlocks a problem like Houdini.
The best-equipped philologist on Earth,
Contini, in my view – for what that's worth –
Was sent by providence to heal the schism
That sunders scholarship from criticism.)

The obstacle for Dante, claims the Prof.,
Lay in the strictness of the *terza rima*.
The old New Style perforce was written off,
Or rather, written up: the lyric dreamer
Got sharper with his tongue, became a schemer
Co-opting dozens of vocabularies
Into a language that forever varies

Yet in its forward pressure never falters –
A rhythmic pulse that somehow stays the same
For all its concrete detail always alters.
A form he would, when young, have thought a game
Had now the status of a sacred flame,
A fertile self-renewing holy trinity
Designed to give his Comedy divinity.

It worked, too, as I'm sure you have detected
Now that you're trained to read the Eyetie tongue.
At least I hope you have. If you've neglected
Your Dante when like mine your wife's among
His foremost female fans, you should be hung,
Or hanged. At getting grammar through to students
Your Judy's letter perfect, like my Prudence,

She's perfect in all ways . . . but I digress.
However true, it's crass to call one's spouse
A paragon of loving comeliness
Who yet rates alpha double plus for nous
While still remaining keen to clean the house.
A paradox worth pondering upon:
We each loathed Academe, yet wed a Don.

I don't know what my wife's at, half the time:
Locked up with microfilms of some frail text
Once copied from a copy's copy. I'm
Dead chuffed as well as miffed to be perplexed,
Contented neither of us has annexed
The other's field. Though it's conceited-sounding,
We Jameses think each other quite astounding.

I'd like to be back there at home right now,
Receiving from my helpmeet a fond look.
But here we Aussies are, rehearsing how
To quell with every cheap trick in the book
The Castle's evil Oriental cook –
A role played by a lithe and slightly spooky
Karate-ka 5th Dan, Meijii Suzuki.

He is (ah, but you twigged!) a Japanese.
I've never seen a man more fit or fleeter.
That guy can pull your teeth out with his knees
And kick the whiskers off a passing cheetah.
To Bazza's pals (me, Scrotum, Tazz and Skeeter)
Whom Meijii smites (the script says) hip and thigh,
He looks like at least seven samurai.

Perhaps propelled by an electric motor
His flying feet can draw blood like a knife.
His brain by Sony, body by Toyota,
This bloke's the Yellow Peril to the life:
And yet, a man of peace. In place of strife
He puts a focused force of meditation
That transcendentalises aggravation.

A day of learning not to get too near him
Can leave you breathless. Think I'll hit the sack.
I'd like to tell the lad that, while I fear him,
I love the way he works; but there's a lack
In our communication. Keeping track
Of when he plans to lash out without warning
Has knackered me for now. More in the morning.

                    *   *   *

Another day since I began composing
These verses in spare moments has now passed,
And here's a whole free hour I can't spend dozing:
A chance to see the gallery at last.
It's early closing, though: so, breathing fast,
I sprint to the museum, pay 10 pee,
Race up the stairs, and Pow! Guess what I see:

Enough to make a man burst into tears.
Renoir's 'Parisian Girl'. A lilting dream
He painted, to the year, one hundred years
Ago. Deep storm-cloud blue and double cream,
Her clothes and skin are eddies in a stream
Of brush-strokes on a shawl of pastel silk,
A peacock-feather spectrum drowned in milk.

These rhapsodies in blue are his best things,
The style in which he really gets it on.
The Jeu de Paume has one that fairly sings –
A portrait of his kids, including Jean,
The boy who, when Pierre-Auguste was gone,
Became Renoir – whose pictures, as it proved,
Were just as human, just as great, and moved.

Even unto the second generation
Sheer genius descended, fully-fashioned.
A transference that rates as a sensation:
That kind of baton-change is strictly rationed.
For which our gratitude should be impassioned –
If artistry, like money, ran in blood-lines
You very soon would find those blood-lines dud lines

[73]

Or dead lines. But we ought to leave to P. B.
Medawar the Nature–Nurture number:
I'm sure he's in the right. I'd get the heebie-
Jeebies reading Eysenck, except slumber
Has always supervened. They're loads of lumber,
Those figures meant to prove genetic strains
Determine your inheritance of brains,

For nobody escapes the play of chance.
The contract's binding: you have got the part.
You have to mime and juggle, sing and dance,
And when you think you've got the role by heart
Some idiot rewrites it from the start.
Nor is there, when your scenes run into trouble,
A volunteer prepared to be your double.

Tomorrow we're to film the kung-fu brawl.
Its imminence has got me feeling cagey,
Not least because I'm due to take a fall.
I'm worried (a) my acting might look stagey,
And (b) I'll have my head caved in by Meijii.
Cavorting with delight at making flicks
He'll get his thrills, but I might get his kicks.

The fight-arranger is my chum Alf Joint,
The Stunt-Man King (he did *Where Eagles Dare*,
The caper on the cable-car). The point,
Says Alf, in flying safely through the air
Is landing with some energy to spare
So as to ease the shock of logs and boulders
By smart use of one's padded arms and shoulders.

'You're falling about two foot six,' they've said.
When put like that it doesn't sound like much.
The catch, though, is I'm landing on my head.
My first film role will need the tumbler's touch
Or else end on a stretcher or a crutch.
From Alf, who's done an eighty-times-as-high dive,
I can't expect much sympathy when *I* dive.

This could be the last stanza of my poem.
I'll scrawl a coda if I come up smiling,
But now I have to get out there and show 'em.
I find the idea nowhere near beguiling:
Suzuki's leg looks like a concrete piling.
But Hell, let's go. What's coping with a killer
To someone who wrote monthly for Karl Miller?

*   *   *

Per ardua ad astra. I survived!
The scrap went perfectly. In Panavision
It should seem like the Day of Wrath's arrived.
My nose and Meijii's toe faked their collision
And I, without a second's indecision,
Collapsed. I toast (in Coke) success (comparative)
And him who wrote my role into the narrative,

Bruce Beresford. From birth, my oldest mate
Was destined to call 'Action', 'Cut' and 'Print'
And 'Stop' and 'What went wrong? You fainted late,'
'You died too soon,' 'No good, I saw you squint,'
And (this to me) 'You're mugging. Make like Clint
Or Kirk or Burt. Don't even bat an eyelid:
Then, when the kick comes, crumple the way I did.'

That we would see in letters five feet high
His name one day spread shining in the gloom
Preceded with the words 'Directed by' –
To doubt that prospect there was never room.
He had the screenplay ready in the womb.
He was (he'll know I say it without unction)
By nature built for one creative function.

Alas, not true for us. We're several-sided;
I to a certain, you to a large, degree.
The age is vanished when we might have prided
Ourselves on that. Karl Marx said history
Will get a re-run, but as parody.
The Universal Man won't be returning.
Too bad. But as I write, the castle's burning:

[75]

Our week in Wales will finish with this shot.
The clapper-board has clapped its final clap.
Sighs. Tears. Farewells. You know the bit. The lot.
We'll soon hear, barring unforeseen mishap,
The first assistant calling, 'It's a wrap.'
Of our last day, this is the day's last light
When darkest daylight shades to lightest night –

The time the film crew calls the golden hour.
The castle quakes. The FX flames leap higher.
We rescue Edna Everage from the tower
And super the end titles on the fire.
The heavy croaks. Our triumph is entire.
It's time to say, 'Nuff said.' You don't mind, do you?
I'll post this now, then try to beat it to you.

To Martin Amis:
a letter from Indianapolis

Dear Mart, I write you from a magic spot.
The dullsville capital of Indiana
At this one point, for this one day, has got
Intensity in every nut and spanner.
Soon now the cars will sing their vast Hosannah
And pressure will produce amazing grace.
Drake-Offenhauser! A. J. Foyt's bandanna!
Velazquez painting Philip at the chase
Saw something like these colours, nothing like this race.

Ten-thirty. Half an hour before the start.
The press-box at the Brickyard is up high.
We sit here safely, emperors set apart,
And kibbitz down as those about to die
Cry *Morituri* . . . Yes, but so am I,
And so are you, though not now. When we're older.
Where death will be the last thing we defy,
These madmen feel it perching on their shoulder:
The tremble of the heat is tinged with something colder.

But that's enough of talk about the weather.
To rail against the climate's not good form.
My subject ought to be the latest feather
Protruding from your cap. I mean the Maugham.
I offer you, through gritted teeth, my warm
Congratulations on another coup.
Success for you's so soon become the norm,
Your fresh young ego might be knocked askew.
A widespread fear, I find. Your father thinks so too.

The prize's terms dictate an expedition
To distant lands. That makes you Captain Kirk
Of Starship *Enterprise*. Your Five-Year Mission:
To Boldly Go etcetera. You can't shirk
The challenge. This award's not just a perk:
Queer Maugham's £500 are meant to send
Your mind in search of fodder for your work
Through any far-flung way you care to wend.
Which means, at present rates, a fortnight in Southend,

So choosing Andalusia took nerve.
It's certainly some kind of foreign part.
A bit close-flung, perhaps, but it will serve
To show you the left knee, if not the heart,
Of European Culture. It's a start.
Like Chesterfield advising his young son
(Who didn't, I imagine, give a fart)
I'm keen to see your life correctly run.
You can't just arse around forever having fun.

The day's work here began at 6 a.m.
The first car they pumped full of gasoline
And wheeled out looked unworldly, like a LEM.
A Mass was said. 'The Lord is King.' The scene
Grew crammed with every kind of clean machine.
An Offenhauser woke with shrieks and yells.
The heart-throb Dayglo pulse and Duco preen
Of decals filled the view with charms and spells
As densely drawn and brilliant as the Book of Kells.

BORG WARNER. BARDAHL. 'Let the Earth rejoice.'
'May Christ have mercy.' LODESTAR. OLSONITE.
America exults with sponsored voice
From Kitty Hawk to ultra-Lunar flight.
RAYBESTOS. GULF. Uptight and out of sight!
The Cape. BELL HELMETS. Gemini. Apollo!
Jay Gatsby put his faith in the green light.
Behold his dream, and who shall call it hollow?
What genius they have, what destinies they follow!

The big pre-race parade comes down the straight
While hardened press-men lecherously dote
On schoolgirl majorettes all looking great
In boots and spangled swimsuits. Flags denote
Their provenance. The band from Terre Haute
Is called the Marching Patriots. Purdue
Has got a drum so big it needs a float.
And now the Dancing Bears come prancing through,
Their derrières starred white and striped with red and blue.

From Tucson, Kokomo and Tuscaloosa,
From over the state line and far away,
Purveying the complete John Philip Sousa
The kids have come for this one day in May
To show the watching world the USA
Survives and thrives and still knows how to cock its
Snoot. Old Uncle Sam is A-OK –
He's strutting with bright buttons and high pockets.
Hail, Tiger Band from Circleville! Broad Ripple Rockets!

Objectively, perhaps, they do look tatty.
This continent's original invaders
Were not, however, notably less ratty.
Torpedoes in tin hats and leather waders,
Hard bastards handing beads around like traders –
Grand larceny in every squeak and rattle.
The whole deal was a nightmare of Ralph Nader's,
A corporate racket dressed up as a battle:
The locals kissed the Spaniard's foot or died like cattle.

The choice between the New World and the Old
I've never found that clear, to tell the truth.
Tradition? Yes indeed, to that I hold:
These bouncing brats from Des Moines and Duluth
Seem short of every virtue except youth.
But really, was there that much more appeal
In stout Cortez's lack of ruth and couth
Simply because it bore the papal seal?
It's art that makes the difference, and Art means the Ideal:

Velazquez (*vide supra*) for example.
You're visiting the Prado, I presume?
Well, when you do, you'll find a healthy sample
Abstracted from his *œuvre* from womb to tomb.
The key works line one giant, stunning room:
Group portraits done in and around the Court
Whose brilliance cleans your brains out like a broom.
Bravura, yes. But products, too, of thought:
An inner world in which the Kings ruled as they ought,

Not as they did. His purpose wasn't flattery
Or cravenly to kiss the royal rod.
He just depicted the assault and battery
Of Habsburg policies as acts of God,
Whose earthly incarnation was the clod
That currently inhabited the throne.
He deified the whole lot on his tod,
Each royal no-no, nincompoop and crone.
Great Titian was long gone. Velazquez was alone.

Alone, and hemmed about by mediocrities
(Except for once when Rubens came to town),
He must have felt as singular as Socrates
But didn't let the pressure get him down.
He slyly banked his credit with the Crown
Until he was allowed a year abroad
(In Rome, of course. In Venice he might drown.)
To raise his sights by study. An award
The King well knew would be a hundredfold restored.

Conquistadores in their *armadura*
The drivers now are standing by their cars.
Unholy soldiers (but in purpose purer),
They look as if they're shipping out for Mars.
It's hard to tell the rookies from the stars:
When suited-up and masked, they seem the same.
White skin-grafts are the veteran's battle-scars.
For A. J. Foyt the searing price of fame
Was branded round his mouth the day he ate the flame.

A year back young Swede Savage swallowed fire.
He took six months to die. It goes to show
How hot it is inside a funeral pyre
And just how hard a row the drivers hoe.
I can't believe they're in this for the dough.
The secret's not beyond, but in, the fear:
A focal point of grief they get to know
Some other place a million miles from here –
The dream Hart Crane once had, to travel in a tear.

Eleven on the dot. The zoo gets hit
By lightning. Lions whelp and panthers panic.
The fastest qualifiers quit the pit
No more than hipbone-high to a mechanic
And take the track. The uproar is Satanic.
By now the less exalted have departed,
But still the sound is monumental, manic.
Librarians would hear it broken-hearted.
And this lap's just for lining up. They haven't started.

Around the speedway cruising on the ton
(Which means for Indy cars, they're nearly stalling)
They blaze away like spaceships round the Sun –
A shout of thunder like Valhalla falling.
(I'm running out of epithets: it's galling.
I've never heard a noise like this before.)
They're coming round again. And it's appalling –
The moment when you can't stand any more,
The green light goes! Geronimo! Excelsior!

It's gangway for the new apocalypse!
They're racing at two hundred miles an hour!
The likelier contenders get to grips
Like heavy cavalry berserk with power
And three-time-winner Foyt already rips
Away to lead the field by half a mile
As up the ante goes. Down go the chips.
No one but Rutherford can match that style,
And he starts too far back. I'll tell you in a while

[81]

The way it all comes out, but now I've got
To set this screed aside and keep a check
From lap to lap on who, while driving what,
Gets hits by whom or ends up in a wreck.
A half a thousand miles is quite a trek –
Though even as I'm jotting down this line
A. J.'s got someone breathing down his neck . . .
Yes, Rutherford's MacLaren, from row nine,
Has moved up more than twenty places. Heady wine!

Since Johnny Rutherford is from Fort Worth
And Foyt from Houston, they are Texans twain:
The both of them behind the wheel since birth,
The both of them straight-arrow as John Wayne.
This thing they're doing's technically insane
And yet there's no denying it's a thrill:
For something fundamental in the brain
Rejoices in the daring and the skill.
The heart is lifted, even though the blood may chill.

It's SOME TIME LATER. On the victory dais
Glad Rutherford gets kissed and plied with drink.
It looks a bit like supper at Emmaus.
Unceasing worship's damaging, I think:
One's standards of self-knowledge tend to sink.
I'd like to try it, though, I must confess.
Perhaps a little bit. Not to the brink.
Nor would that heap of lolly cause distress:
Three hundred thousand dollars – not a penny less.

Until half-way, the prize belonged to Foyt.
His pretty GILMORE RACING ketchup-red
Coyote skated flatter than a quoit,
The maestro lying down as if in bed.
He only led by inches, but he led –
Until his turbo-charger coughed white smoke.
The car kept running quickly while it bled,
But finally – black flag. For Foyt, no joke:
Unless he had his money on the other bloke.

The Coming Boy on his eleventh try
At winning the '500' finished first.
A perfect journey. No one had to die.
On looking back, I think about the worst
Catastrophe was that an engine burst.
The empty Brickyard bakes in silent heat,
The quarter-million race-fans have dispersed,
And I have got a deadline I must meet:
I have to tell the story of the champion's defeat.

Velazquez was ennobled in the end.
(Old Philip, fading fast, could not refuse
The final accolade to such a friend.)
His background was examined for loose screws
(Against the blood of craftsmen, Moors or Jews
Bureaucracy imposed a strict embargo)
And in a year or so came the good news,
Together with the robes and wealthy cargo
They used to hang around a Knight of Santiago.

Encumbered thus, he sank into the grave.
The man is dead. The artist is alive.
For lonely are the brilliant, like the brave –
Exactly like, except their deeds survive.
My point (it's taken ages to arrive)
Is simply this: enjoy the adulation,
But meanwhile take a tip from Uncle Clive
And amplify your general education.
There's more than literature involved in cultivation.

Tomorrow in the London afternoon
I'll miss your stubby, Jaggerish appearance
And wish you back in Fleet Street very soon.
Among the foremost ranks of your adherents
I'm vocal to the point of incoherence
When totting up your qualities of mind.
You've even got the rarest: perseverance.
A wise adviser ought to be resigned,
Unless he keeps the pace hot, to being left behind.

'We're given Art in order not to perish
Faced with the Truth.' Or words to that effect.
An apophthegm of Nietzsche's which I cherish:
He sees how these two areas connect
Without conceding that they intersect.
Enough for now. Go easy, I implore you.
It all abides your questing intellect.
The Heritage of Culture, I assure you,
Like everything, you lucky sod, is all before you.

To Pete Atkin: a letter from Paris

Trapped here in Paris, Pete, to shoot some scenes
Which end a film that's tied me up for weeks,
I've lost track of what what I'm doing means.
The streets of the Étoile are filled like creeks
By driving rain that blinds our fine machines.
We squat indoors, unprepossessing freaks
Made up as rough-cast hoboes of both sexes,
Surrounded by sun-guns and Panaflexes.

Our schedule's gone to Hades. Meanwhile you
Have gone to Scotland, there to make the rounds
Of clubs and halls to introduce our new
Collection of low-down yet highbrow sounds –
A sacrifice I hail. And so, in lieu
Of calls that would be tricky and cost pounds,
I'm scrawling you this missive in *ottava*,
A form I like Fields like Mocha-Java.

That Byron incarnates Don Juan in it
Should make it suicide to use again.
This note would end before I could begin it
Were I to dwell on that least pinched of men
(Who turned these stanzas out at two a minute)
And bring to mind the splendour of his pen,
The sheer *élan*, the lift, the loose-limbed jollity –
Yes, blue – but true blue, right? Legit. Star quality.

A strength that helps to prove these verse-form shapes
(Home-spun or else, like this one now, imported)
Are far from being decorative drapes
Deployed to prettify some ill-assorted
Conceptions best half-hidden: the gap gapes
Between the thought and deed (and drawn and quartered
Lies your result) if that's your estimation.
These strict schemes are a kind of cogitation

In their own right. Without them, no real thinking
Beyond the surface flotsam in the skull
Can happen. It takes more than steady drinking
To stop creative writers being dull.
Their gifts they'll soon find upside-down and sinking
If discipline has not first keeled the hull.
For all true poets rhyme must equal reason
And formlessness be just a form of treason.

So no surprise you were the man for me,
Though others sang with much more cute a voice.
Approval was no matter of degree
But absolute. There was no other choice.
Our linking up was pure necessity,
As certainly as Rolls had need of Royce.
I viewed you, while the Footlights shouted Encore,
The way one Goncourt viewed the other Goncourt.

This kid, I mused, knows how to grasp the nettle.
With him the formal urge is automatic.
He's lamped the fact that only heat moulds metal
Or pressure makes the lyrical dramatic.
One's syllables would soon attain fine fettle
If tethered to his notes, be less erratic;
One's lexical pizzazz avoid fatuity
Attached to that melodic perspicuity.

We met, we talked of Bean and Brute and Bird
And Rabbit. You were full of praise for Trane.
We both thought early Miles had had the word
But (now I know this went against the grain)
I thought he later lost it. Had I heard
Of Archie Shepp? Yes. Good? No. Right: inane.
Our views were close, and on one salient thing
Inseparably united – Duke was King.

Of 'Main Stem', ' "C" Jam Blues' and 'Cottontail',
Of 'Take the "A" Train', 'In a Mellotone'
And 'Harlem Air Shaft' we took turns to wail
The solos so definitively blown
By sidemen somewhere in the age of sail –
The pre-war Forties, when Duke stood alone,
His every disc a miniature immensity,
The acme of schooled ease and spacious density.

It soon turned out you thought post-Presley pop
As real as jazz. This wheeze was new to me
And caught my sense of fitness on the hop:
I loved the stuff, but come now, seriously . . .
Hold on, though. My beliefs howled to a stop
And chose reverse. With one bound, Jack was free.
If rock struck me as fruitful, lively, good –
Why not get in and gain a livelihood?

The Broadway partnership of words and tune
Had been dissolved by pop, which then reverted
In all good faith to rhyming moon with June,
Well pleased with the banalities it blurted.
Those speech defects would need attention soon.
Gillespie and Kildare, in aim concerted,
We got started . . . but enough now in that strain:
The whole a.m. has just gone down the drain.

I'm sure the cost of sitting here is frightening
And days ago it ceased to be much fun.
Though, as we lunch, the sky might just be lightening:
This afternoon we could get something done.
And now the outlook's definitely brightening,
So more from the location. I must run.
We've just been told to grab a cab and ride out
To some guy called Quatorze's country hideout.

*   *   *

The weather's cleared. We're filming at Versailles,
Palatial residence of Sun King Louis,
Where everything is landscaped save the sky
And even that seems strangely free of *pluie*
For this one day at least. I find that I
Am sneakily inclined to murmur 'phooey'
When faced with all this Classical giganticism:
In fact it almost makes me like Romanticism.

Proportion, yes: the joint's got that to burn.
Sa regularity of window arch,
Ses ranks of cornucopia and urn.
Those balustrades like soldiers on the march!
Those gardens, haunt of robot coot and hern!
The whole confection fairly reeks of starch:
A dude ranch frozen with neurotic tension,
It chills the very notion of dissension.

And that was what *le Roi Soleil* was after,
Without a doubt. His absolutist frown
Is there in every pediment and rafter,
A stare of disapproval beating down
Propensities to any form of laughter
Beyond the courtly hollow kind. The Crown
Made sure to keep this 4-star barracks filled
With dupes who thought they danced but really drilled.

Grim-jawed solemnity may have its worth
But geniality is just as serious
And *gravitas* is half-deaf without mirth.
I don't mean one should roll around delirious
But art must take the air, not hug the earth –
Authoritative needn't mean imperious.
To preach cold concepts like the golden section
Is over-mightily to seek perfection.

We should be glad, then, that we work in rock
Whose mark for ordered symmetry is zero.
Its *cognoscenti*, talking total cock
Concerning slack-mouthed bitch or dildoed hero,
Combine the thickness of a mental block
With all the musicality of Nero:
And yet despite their IQs in two figures
They've sussed out where the only decent gig is.

In liking anti-intellectualism
They're wrong, but right to value simple verve.
A long way gone in pale eclecticism,
Like all those nostrums that no longer serve
(Vedanta, Social Credit, Pelmanism)
The classical succession's lost its nerve –
Or else it shrieks an *avant-gardiste* foolery
That makes the average rock song shine like joolery.

But here the shine's gone off a hard half-day:
We're wrapping up with no shots left to do.
Inside a camera car I'm borne away
Along a six-lane speedway to St Cloud,
Where signboards set to lead non-Frogs astray
Now send us back Versailles-wards. Sacray bloo.
Our pub will keep a meal, though . . . Bloody Hell!
No food: we have to work tonight as well.

        *   *   *

Throughout the evening's shooting in Pigalle
I marvel, as the red lights glow infernally,
That they can pull down places like Les Halles
When (rain or shine, nocturnally, diurnally,
Uncaring if you snigger, sneer or snarl)
Grim tat and tit dance cheek by jowl eternally
In *this* dump. What a drag! But its survival
Is no surprise if taste's its only rival.

[89]

Alone at last, I'm much too tired to sleep
(A hemistitch from Lorenz Hart. You tumbled?)
The drapes down-soft, the wall-to-wall knee-deep,
My hotel bedroom ought to leave me humbled.
By rights I should conk out without a peep,
But can't. The boys who did the décor fumbled:
It's just too scrumptious to be borne, too peachy.
They've ladled on an acre too much chi-chi.

The Gauche and not the Droite's the Rive for me.
To kip beneath plush quilts is not the same
As gazing *sur les toits* of that Paree
They fly behind the garret window-frame,
Heraldic as France Ancient's fleur-de-lys,
To charm you through Act I of *La Bohème* –
Unless I've got Parnasse mixed up with Martre.
(You know I still can't tell those Monts apartre?)

So much for taste, then, and the same goes double
For those more recent phantoms, such as Youth.
As clear and brilliant as the tiny bubble
That canopies a baby's first front tooth,
There swells through times of sloth and troughs of trouble
The artist's one eternal, guiding truth –
Ars longa, vita brevis. Is that Horace?
It could be someone weird, like William Morris.

*　　*　　*

I'm writing half-way up the Eiffel Tower
While knocking back a rich *café au lait*.
We've been at work this high about an hour
And here my part will end, at noon today.
It gives a heady, Zeus-like sense of power
To watch, from *au-dessus de la mêlée*,
The myriad formiculant mere mortals
Who circumvest this crazy structure's portals.

Much earlier, and lovely in the dawn,
The gardens of the Louvre were full of mist.
The Tuileries lay like a smoking lawn
As I, my trusty notebook in my fist,
Saw Paris come unfolded like a fawn
And glitter like a powdered amethyst –
Whereat I felt, involved in her fragility,
A thumping streak of tough bitch durability.

We're all aware of how the continuity
Of Western culture's frazzled to a thread.
It doesn't take a soothsayer's acuity
To see the whole shebang might wind up dead.
One's sorely tempted to, in perpetuity,
Give up the struggle and go back to bed:
And yet Tradition, though we can't renew it,
Demands we add our certain something to it

No matter what. I leave from Charles de Gaulle
At Roissy this p.m. S-F HQ!
The planes feed in a cluster, like a shoal
Of mutant carp stuck nose to nose with glue
Around a doughnut in whose abstract hole
Aphasic humans escalating through
Translucent pipelines linking zones to domes
Seem pastel genes in giant chromosomes.

And that's the future, baby. Like the past
It's flowing, but unlike it it flows faster.
Ici Paris, below me. Will it last?
A heap of ageing bricks and wood and plaster –
Bombe glacée with one atomic blast.
A single finger's tremble from disaster.
But then, who isn't? So what else is new?
See you in London: there's a lot to do.

To Prue Shaw:
a letter from Cambridge

I miss you. As I settle down to write,
   Creating for my forearm room to rest,
   I see the hard grey winter evening light
Is scribbled on with lipstick in the west
   As just another drowsy Cambridge day
   Discreetly shines and shyly looks its best
Before, with eyeballs glazed, it slides away
   And slips into a night's sleep deeper still,
   Where Morpheus holds undisputed sway
Throughout the weary academic mill –
   An atmosphere of cosy somnolence
   I hope that I can summon up the will
To counteract. I'm striving to condense
   Within the *terza rima* my ideas
   Concerning us, the arts and world events.
I shake my skull, which for the moment clears,
   And shape a line to say that minus you
   I'm lonelier than Hell and bored to tears:
Then slumber paints my eyelids thick with glue.
   Uncertainty bemuses. Somewhere round
   Lake Garda you've got lost and left no clue.
The post is void of cards, the phone of sound.
   If you were elsewhere than in Italy
   I'd start a hue and cry to get you found,
But as things are I think it best to be
   More circumspect. The blower's on the blink
   Across the strike-bound north from sea to sea,
And Heaven only knows the waste of ink
   Involved in trusting letters to the mail.
   The ship of state is getting set to sink
Again. (The poor thing never learned to sail.)
   Italia! Poverina! Yes, and yet
   The place's old enchantments never fail
To work their subtle wiles. You'll not forget,
   I'm sure, when passing ice-cold Sirmione,
   The way we used to swim and not get wet

In water soft and warm as *zabaglione*.
   The titles to the olive groves and palaces
   Catullus walked with courtesan and crony
In our time were Onassis's and Callas's,
   But as you stood hip-deep in liquid air
   I thought the moment sweet past all analysis
And thanked the pagan Gods I knew were there
   (The sunset stretched a ladder of gold chains
   Across the lake) that they'd been so unfair
In handing you the beauty *and* the brains.
   An egocentric monster then as now
   I graciously resolved to keep my gains
By staying near you, never thinking how
   You might not co-divide that deep esteem.
   Unwarrantedly dry of palm and brow
I wed you, in due course. Today I dream
   Of what I would, if I had missed the boat
   Undoubtedly have undergone. A scream
Of retroactive anguish rends my throat.
   That physicist from Stockholm you refused,
   The one who tried to buy you a fur coat:
To think of the affection I abused!
   Now here was this attractive, well-heeled bloke,
   Whose talk of synchrotrons kept you amused,
Whose china-white Mercedes – Holy smoke!
   What made me certain he should get the grief
   And I the joy? I swear I almost croak
From apprehension mingled with relief
   Recalling how I flirted with defeat.
   It's only now I think myself a thief –
Of his luck and your time. You were to meet
   Yet brighter prospects later. I still won.
   I had a system nobody could beat.
I flailed about and called my folly fun
   For years and even then was not too late:
   The threads that joined us were as strongly spun
As your forgivingness of me was great.
   I wonder that your heart has not grown numb,
   So long you've had (or felt you've had) to wait
For my unthinking fondness to become

A love for you like yours for me. The fault
   Is all mine if it has, for being dumb.
I'd have no comeback under Heaven's vault
   – my only plea could be *è colpa mia*,
   A hanging head, and tears that tasted salt –
If you should fade from my life like *la Pia*.
   But you have not, so I shall for the nonce
   Eschew this droning form of logorrhoea
Which feeds upon what might have happened once
   And hasten to give thanks that you and I,
   Like Verdi and Strepponi or the Lunts,
Seem apt, so far at least, to give the lie
   To notions that all order falls apart –
   Though giving them as one who would defy
The Gods, yet feels a flutter in his heart.
   Has something happened? Down there, so much can.
   The right wing terrorists are acting smart.
They've thought hard and have come up with a plan:
   To bomb the innocent. Earmarked for death
   Are woman, daughter, child and unarmed man.
From now on no one draws an easy breath.
   Your train ride down to Florence will be like
   Accepting a night's lodging from Macbeth.
I wonder if you'd rather hire a bike?
   Except the roads aren't safe. Well, why not walk?
   You'd thrive on a four hundred mile hike . . .
But no, all this is fearful husband's talk:
   What-might-be acting like what-might-have-been
   To turn my knees to jelly, cheeks to chalk.
No matter how infernal the machine
   Prepared to blow our sheltered lives to bits,
   It would be less than just, indeed obscene,
To harbour the suspicion murder fits
   The Italian national character. Not so.
   As always, most of them live by their wits
Amidst – as, to your cost, you've come to know –
   Administrative chaos. It's a wonder
   That utter barbarism's been so slow
In gaining ground from brouhaha and blunder,
   Yet even when *Fascismo* had its hour

The blood was always upstaged by the thunder.
They held pyjama parties with their power
    Forgetting to wipe out a single race.
    Some blockhead said a bomb was like a flower,
Some communists got booted in the face,
    But no one calls that lapse a Holocaust –
    More like a farce that ended in disgrace,
When men yelled like a racing car's exhaust
    In uniforms adorned with a toy dagger;
    A time when word and meaning were divorced,
Divided by a verbal strut and swagger
    As pompous as a moose's mating call,
    Bombastic as a war dance by Mick Jagger.
But we both know it's not like that at all,
    The eternal Italy, the one that matters.
    The blue-chinned heavies at the costume ball
Whose togs inept explosions blow to tatters
    Are just the international tribe of jerks
    That crop up anywhere, as mad as hatters,
To pistol-whip the poor and cop the perks.
    The real Italians, far from on the make,
    Are makers. Ye shall know them by their works –
To which the guide who brought me wide awake
    Was you, ten years ago. You were my tutor.
    At times you must have thought this a mistake
And wished me elsewhere, or at least astuter.
    I paced our tiny rented room in Rome,
    I crackled like an overtaxed computer
And used my nerve-wracked fingers for a comb,
    Attempting to construe *Inferno* Five.
    It took so long I wanted to go home
But comprehension started to arrive
    At last. I saw the lovers ride the storm
    And felt the pulse which brought the dead alive.
For sheer intensity of lyric form
    I'd never read that stretch of verse's peer.
    You said such things, with Dante, were the norm.
You proved it, as we read on for a year.
    And so it was our Galahad, that book,
    As well as one ordained to make it clear

How art and intellect are king and rook
    And not just man and wife and guest and host –
    They link together like an eye and hook
While each moves through the other like a ghost.
    Both interpenetrate inside the mind
    And, in creation, nothing matters most –
By Dante these great facts are underlined,
    Made incandescent like a sunlit rose.
    My clenched fist thumped my forehead. I'd been blind!
Awaking from a Rip Van Winkle doze
    I realised I'd been groping in the gloom,
    Not even good at following my nose.
A knowing bride had schooled a clumsy groom:
    Belated, crude, but strong, his urge to learn
    Began there, in that shoe-box of a room –
A classic eager dim-wit doomed to burn
    The candle at both ends while, head in hands,
    He mouths what he can only just discern
And paragraphs twice read half understands.
    To Petrarch's verses and to Croce's thought
    We moved on later. Etiquette demands
I don't go on about the books we bought
    In all those second-hand shops we infested.
    I've never mastered grammar as I ought.
My scraps of erudition aren't digested.
    But still I've grown, drawn out by what I've read,
    More cosmopolitan – well, less sequestered.
(Our old friend Goethe, writing in his head,
    Would tap out stresses on his girlfriend's spine.
    Gorblimey, talk about Technique in Bed!
Urbanity on *that* scale's not my line.
    I must admit, however, that at times
    I found my brain, as well as fogged with wine,
Inopportunely chattering with rhymes.)
    And then there were the canvases and frescoes,
    Cascading like a visual change of chimes
Or stacked ten-deep like racks of tins in Tesco's
    All over Rome and Naples, Florence, Venice . . .
    I felt like a research group of UNESCO's
Investigating some microbic menace:

[96]

To sort it out, life wasn't long enough.
It just went on like Rosewall playing tennis.
There wasn't any end to all that stuff.
    An early Raphael, or late Perugino?
    (I haven't got a clue. I'll have to bluff.)
Who sculpted this, Verrocchio or Mino?
    (But who the heck was Mino?) No doubt what
    The banquet would have soon become (a beano
With sickness as the sequel) had you not
    Been there to function as my dietitian;
    Ensuring I'd not try to scoff the lot
But merely taste each phase at its fruition,
    Assimilating gradually, and thus
    Catch up with Europe's civilised tradition –
Which wasn't really a departing bus,
    You argued, but a spirit all around me
    I'd get attuned to if I didn't fuss.
From that time forward every summer found me
    In Florence, where you studied all year long.
    Your diligence continued to astound me.
I went on getting attributions wrong,
    But bit by bit I gained perceptiveness
    As day by day I keenly helped to throng
The galleries, exalted – nothing less –
    By how those fancy lads all worked like slaves
    To make their age so howling a success
Before they rolled, fulfilled, into their graves.
    In Cambridge, night wears on. The evening ending
    Will soon dictate the sleep my system craves.
I'll close. These lines might just be worth the sending
    To Florence, care of Rita at her flat.
    Supposing they get through, they'll wait there, pending
Your safe arrival – and amen to that.
    That city is a place where we were poor.
    In furnished dungeons blacker than your hat
We slept, or failed to, on the concrete floor
    And met the morning's heat chilled to the bone –
    Yet each day we felt better than before
Forgetting what it meant to be alone.
    Well, this is what it means: distracting games

[97]

With tricky rhyme-schemes and – wait, there's the phone.
'Will you accept a call from Mrs James?'
    P.S. You've made this letter obsolete
    But rather than consign it to the flames
I'll send it. For you must admit, my sweet,
    A triple-rhyming verse communication,
    While scarcely ranking as an epic feat,
Deserves perusal by its inspiration.

To Tom Stoppard:
a letter from London

To catch your eye in Paris, Tom,
I choose a show-off stanza from
   Some Thirties play
Forgotten now like Rin Tin Tin.
Was it *The Dog Beneath the Skin*?
   Well, anyway

Its tone survives. The metres move
Through time like paintings in the Louvre
   (Say loov, not loover):
Coherent in their verbal jazz,
They're confident of tenure as
   J. Edgar Hoover.

Pink fairies of the sixth form Left,
Those Ruined Boys at least were deft
   At the actual writing.
Though history scorns all they thought,
The nifty artefacts they wrought
   Still sound exciting.

Distinguishing the higher fliers
Remorselessly from plodding triers
   Who haven't got it,
Such phonic zip bespeaks a knack
Of which no labour hides the lack:
   A child could spot it.

And boy, you've got the stuff in bales –
A Lubitsch-touch that never fails.
   The other guys
Compared to you write lines that float
With all the grace of what gets wrote
   By Ernest Wise.

The Stoppard dramaturgic moxie
Unnerves the priests of orthodoxy:
    We still hear thicks
Who broadcast the opinion freely
Your plays are only sketches really –
    Just bags of tricks.

If dramas do not hammer themes
Like pub bores telling you their dreams
    The dense don't twig.
They want the things they know already
Reiterated loud and steady –
    Drilled through the wig.

From all frivolity aloof,
Those positivist killjoys goof
    Two ways at once:
They sell skill short, and then ignore
The way your works are so much more
    Than clever stunts.

So frictionless a *jeu d'esprit*,
Like Wittgenstein's philosophy,
    Appears to leave
Things as they are, but at the last
The future flowing to the past
    Without reprieve

Endorses everything you've done.
As Einstein puts it, The Old One
    Does not play dice,
And though your gift might smack of luck
Laws guide it, like the hockey puck
    Across the ice.

Deterministic you are not,
However, even by a jot.
    Your sense of form
Derives its casual power to thrill
From operating at the still
    Heart of the storm.

[100]

For how could someone lack concern
Who cared that gentle Guildenstern
    And Rosencrantz
(Or else the same names rearranged
Should those two men be interchanged)
    Were sent by chance

To meet a death at Hamlet's whim
Less grand than lay in store for him,
    But still a death:
A more appalling death, in fact
Than any king's in the Fifth Act –
    Even Macbeth?

In south-east Asia as I type
The carbuncle is growing ripe
    Around Saigon.
The citadels are soon reduced.
The chickens have come home to roost.
    The heat is on,

And we shall see a sickness cured
Which virulently has endured
    These thirty years:
The torturers ran out of jails,
The coffin-makers out of nails,
    Mothers of tears,

While all the Furies and the Fates
Unleashed by the United States
    In Freedom's name
Gave evidence that moral error
Returns in tumult and in terror
    The way it came.

But now the conquerors bring peace.
When everyone is in the police
    There's no unrest.
Except for those who disappear
The People grin from ear to ear –
    Not like the West.

Rejecting both kinds of belief
(Believing only in the grief
   Their clash must bring)
We find to use the words we feel
Adhere most closely to the real
   Means everything.

I like the kind of jokes you tell
And what's more you like mine as well –
   Clear proof of nous.
I like your stylish way of life.
I've thought of kidnapping your wife.
   I like your house.

Success appeals to my sweet tooth:
But finally it's to the truth
   That you defer –
And that's the thing I like the best.
My love to Miri. Get some rest.
   A tout à l'heure.

To Peter Porter: a letter to Sydney

To reach you in the You-Beaut Country, Peter,
Perforce I choose that scheme of rhyme and metre
Most favoured by your master spirit, Pope –
Whose pumiced forms make mine look like soft soap,
Despite the fact that this last fiscal year
Two thousand of my couplets, pretty near,
Have been read out in public – a clear token
The classical tradition's not yet broken,
Just mangled and left twitching in a ditch
By Aussies apt to scratch the fatal itch
That Juvenal and Dr Johnson dubbed
Cacoethes scribendi and well drubbed.
Your friends in London miss you something fierce:
You are the crux of talk like Mildred Pierce.
At Mille Pini or in Bertorelli's
We scriveners still meet to stoke our bellies
And with red wine we toast you *in absentia*
From soup to nuts and so on to dementia.
The grape juice flowing in across our dentures,
Tall tales flow out concerning your adventures.
As fleet of foot and fearless as Phidippides
You are our pioneer in the Antipodes,
A latter-day but no less dauntless Jason
Or Flying Dutchman as played by James Mason.
Vespucci, Tasman, Drake, Cook, Scott, John Glenn –
To those you left behind you're all these men:
The Town's not heard such daydreams of bravado
Since Raleigh sailed in search of El Dorado.
One rumour says that cheap drinks on the plane
Had detrimental impact on your brain:
It's said you smiled a smile like Nat King Cole's
While trying to take over the controls.
Another rumour graphically describes
The shameless way they're plying you with bribes
(A Philistine approach we're sure you'll spurn)

To make your trip a permanent return.
They've offered you £10,000 a year,
We're told, to dwell out there instead of here –
Plus car, two yachts, a house at Double Bay
And Mrs Whitlam in a negligée.
Temptation! You'd not only soon get rich,
Your kids would scarcely need to wear a stitch –
They'd be as brown as berries in two shakes.
Perhaps you ought to up stakes for *their* sakes . . .
To let them share the unexampled wealth
Australia's young are given free – good health.
Good health (i.e., preventive pediatrics)
Provides the punch behind Jeff Thomson's hat-tricks.
Good health ensures the Ashes stay down under.
It lends John Newcombe's smashes extra thunder.
Good health is what puts beefcake on Rod Taylor –
It makes Rolf Harris sound like a loud-hailer.
Good health helps Eddie Charlton score like Bradman
And Sidney Nolan sling paint like a madman.
But vitamins and body-building cereals
Are only some among the raw materials
That go to stuff the bulging cornucopia
Which all wise men now know to be Utopia –
Though once none but the hopeless ever went there
And death was preferable to being sent there.
The tables are well turned. The biter's bitten.
The pit of desperation now is Britain –
Where soon must fall a dark night of the soul
With (HEALEY WARNS) three million on the dole
Unless some pin is found to pierce inflation
And thereby save the pound and thus the nation.
For their own chances loth to give you tuppence,
The British seem concussed by their come-uppance:
Like fearful Pooh and Piglet they keep humming,
But few believe a cure will be forthcoming
That won't make their poor country even poorer –
A bald man getting drunk on hair-restorer.
To say 'So much the better' would be base
As well as out of key and not my place,
And yet, though some might deem the pause a pity,

The slump seems to have saved our favourite city
From being hacked to pieces like King Priam's –
Here by Joe Levy, there by Harry Hyams.
May wasting assets pauperise them both:
They made a graveyard and they called it Growth.
But now it's clear (thank Heaven for small mercies)
The land boom was a siren-song like Circe's
That sapped the system's last remaining vigour
By crooning, 'You must go on getting bigger.'
To which thought there can only be one answer –
A flagrant Harvey Smith, for so must cancer.
Forgive me if that reference to pathology
Offends your deep concern with eschatology –
The Last Things are for you no laughing matter
And there I go reducing them to patter.
You think of death, you've told me, all the time,
And not as a quietus but a crime.
You think of death, you've told me, as a curse
That caps a life of pain with something worse.
You think of death, you've told me, as obscene,
And all your poems show me what you mean,
For your horrific vision would make Goya
Plead mental cruelty and phone his lawyer –
And even Dürer's 'Ritter, Tod und Teufel'
Beside what you evoke looks almost joyful.
A paradox, in view of this, that you,
Of all the London literary crew,
Are much the most authentically elated
By everything great artists have created.
I miss your talk not just because of savouring
Its bracing lack of artificial flavouring,
But also for the way that Grub Street scandal
Is spiced by you with thoughts on Bach and Handel,
And whether the true high-point of humanity
Was Mozart's innocence or Haydn's sanity.
For though your calling's poetry, your passion
Is Music – and I'm cast in the same fashion,
Believing that man's fate, if hardly cherishable,
Through Music may partake of the imperishable.
(A sacrament, I fear, which smacks of heresy

To some of our close friends among the clerisy,
Who can't conceive of anybody needing it –
And stick to writing verse, while rarely reading it.)
Enough. Since this must reach you through the 'Staggers'
Claire Tomalin will look askance and daggers
At claims for space beyond a second column,
So I shall close. Perhaps with something solemn?
Alas, I'm ill-equipped for sounding cryptic.
Besides, I just don't feel apocalyptic!
For all her empty coffers ring like cisterns,
For all her strength now lies with Sonny Liston's,
For all her looming future looks appalling,
Great Britain must for always be enthralling
To anyone who speaks her native tongue.
Turn back, and leave Australia to the young!
Turn back, and push a pencil as you ought!
Turn back! The times are right for rhymed report!
We need you here to help us face the crunch
(Or, failing that, to face the bill for lunch),
Lest in these islands folly govern men
Until the day King Arthur comes again –
And finds, no doubt, his advent greeted warmly
By Jack Jones, Arthur Scargill and Joe Gormley.

To Michael Frayn:
a letter from Leningrad

I

Dear Michael, here in Leningrad
The wind unseasonably chill
For April ought to make me sad,
And yet I feel a heady thrill
To see the white rice in the air
Blown every which way round the square
Before the Winter Palace. Cold
Grey sky sets off the flourished gold
And whipped-cream plaster rococo
Embellishments that help to make
The place look such a birthday cake –
I only wish there were more snow.
Despite the risk of frozen feet
I'd like to see the dream complete.

II

Speaking of feet: they're killing me.
I've walked around the city now
For ages, there's so much to see.
Already I can well see how
Poets, composers, every kind
Of artist thought this town designed
Exclusively so that they might
Be stimulated day and night
To works of genius. I shan't
Pretend to be quite in their league.
Indeed I'd rather plead fatigue
And shirk the challenge, but I can't:
The ghosts of all those gifted men
Are sneering as I suck my pen.

III

The greatest of them all, of course,
Was Pushkin. I'm just halfway through
His masterpiece, but the full force

Of inspiration's only too
Apparent. In all literature
There's no fecundity so pure
As his. Through him the Gods gave tongue
And made damned certain he died young.
So multifarious a voice,
So disciplined a formal sense –
His talent was just too immense.
He had to go. There was no choice.
Like Mozart he was Heaven-sent
And back to Heaven he soon went.

IV

Eugene Onegin! In an hour
I read one stanza. Such compression
Demands all one's attentive power.
Besides, I must make a confession:
My Russian, after months of sweat,
Is really not so hot as yet.
In fact it's pretty poor. As well
As being envious as Hell
Of all your other attributes,
I wish my army hitch had taught
Me tricks of a more taxing sort.
I studied how to polish boots
With spit and spoon. *You* got to know
The lingo of the dreaded foe.

V

We neither of us won the war.
I'm told it sort of went away
When both sides settled for a draw.
Lord Chalfont still has lots to say
About the imminent Red Threat,
But nothing much has happened yet
In global terms. The Warsaw Pact
Intractably remains a fact.
It's hard to see how they could lose,
Our experts warn, should they advance.
Poor NATO wouldn't stand a chance.

They've got more tanks than they can use.
By midday on D-Day Plus One
They'd be in Budleigh Salterton.

VI

But will they risk annihilation?
I don't think anybody knows.
The thought of total devastation
If ever harsh words come to blows
Still keeps the Super Powers in check.
Better to wring each other's neck
At second hand, on battlegrounds
Where losses can be kept in bounds.
When ideologies collide
They tend to choose exotic places
Where folk with ethnic-looking faces
Don't mind committing suicide,
Or anyway don't seem to. Thus
It's all thrashed out without much fuss.

VII

Meanwhile the vast USSR
Grows ever stronger and more bored.
The ceaseless struggle rages far
Away, in little lands abroad.
The Marxist-Leninist ideal
At home long since became as real
As it could ever be. The State
Takes charge of everybody's fate
From womb to tomb. Complete control
Is exercised on all resources.
The harnessing of natural forces
By now includes the human soul.
What you may do or even dream
Is all laid down by the regime,

VIII

Which should have no more use for terror.
The People now are too well drilled
To contemplate embracing error.
Assent's so thoroughly instilled
That new directives are obeyed
Before they've even been displayed
On all those billboards and red flags
Beneath which every building sags.
Nobody sane could see the need
For harsher methods than this thick
Miasma of bad rhetoric.
The masses long ago agreed
That inner freedom makes no sense.
Which only leaves the Dissidents –

IX

Who go through several kinds of Hell
In special clinics where the drugs
That make them ill instead of well
Are forced upon them, not by thugs,
But qualified psychiatrists.
It's one of history's little twists:
The sane are classified insane
And rather than relieving pain
The doctors cause it. Strange, but true –
When those with preternatural guts
Are first of all defined as nuts,
Then made so – but that's Marx for you:
To put the future beyond doubt
What must be must be brought about.

X

The common run of folk, meanwhile,
Can feel comparatively safe
From decimation Stalin-style.
Their bonds, though still strong, do not chafe
As proudly they with one accord
March asymptotically toward
That feast of dubious delights

Zinoviev calls the Yawning Heights –
A Workers' Paradise on Earth
Which has no use for abstract thought.
Fantastically good at sport
A new mankind has come to birth,
A race that stands a whole head taller –
Except the head's a trifle smaller.

XI

Useless to ask what might have been
Had things stayed roughly as they were.
October 1917
Made certain nothing could occur
Save transformation. History's tide –
Which Spengler said we have to ride
Or else go under – ran its course
With hypermetamorphic force
Until no links were left to sever.
All ties were broken with the past.
No going back. The die was cast
And everything was changed for ever.
How strange, in that case, we should feel
Those days to be so much more real

XII

Than these. Yet really not so strange,
For nothing dates like human dreams
Of Heaven. Terrified of change,
The Russia of the present seems
An embolism. Time forgot
To flow, and stopped, and formed a clot.
There's next to nowt in the whole place –
Including rockets aimed at space –
That wouldn't be there anyway
Had Lenin failed to catch his train.
Suppose he'd chosen to remain
In Zurich, who can really say
His country would not now be strong?
Perhaps he got the whole thing wrong

XIII

And simply blasted in the bud
What might have been a brilliant flower.
Perhaps in shedding so much blood
To gain unchallengeable power
He stopped what was just getting started
And left his country broken-hearted,
With what result we now all know –
The Gulag Archipelago.
Too black a thought with which to end
This letter, and besides, I'm too
Aware that I'm addressing you –
A master of the light touch. Friend,
Forgive my solemn voice of doom.
I aimed at gaiety, not gloom,

XIV

But somehow lost my mirth. Mistake.
It's boorish to parade one's grief
And weep for a whole country's sake,
Assuming it's lost all belief
In human decency. The fact
Remains that, though the deck is stacked
Against them, none the less the just
Are born and win each other's trust.
Nadezhda Mandelstam has said
The truth still comes back from the grave
And she should know. I think I'll waive
What rights I have to mourn the dead.
I'm better at the kind of tears
I cried when seeing *Donkey's Years*.

XV

Besides, I like it here. I've seen
The Peter-Paul and the Tsars' tombs.
I've stared at the Bronze Horseman, been

Through all the Hermitage's rooms.
I've seen the Empress Catherine's clock –
A ten-foot wingspan gold peacock
Some Grand Duke thought the kind of gift
That might convey his general drift.
I've seen . . . But there seems little point,
Here in this Window on the West,
In telling you what you know best.
You've been here and you've cased the joint,
Liking to know whereof you speak.
Good principle. See you next week.

To Craig Raine: a letter from Biarritz

Dear Craig, I've brought your books down to the sea
In order to catch up with what you've done
Since first I gasped at your facility
For writing Martian postcards home. The sun
Illuminates *The Onion, Memory*
Two pages at a time. The beach girls run
With naked bosoms on my low horizon
And yet yours are the lines I've got my eyes on.

Not all the time perhaps, but none the less
It's fair to say I'm utterly drawn in.
When praising your alchemical prowess
One hardly knows the best place to begin.
Your similes are struck with such success
At least one bard has called your gift a sin.
You spot resemblances with a precision
Not normally conferred by human vision.

What I admire and envy most, however,
Is your unflinching hunger for the real.
Proportionate you are but pallid never.
With strength of knee unknown to the genteel
You push on with your passionate endeavour
To sweep aside the veil of the ideal
And view the actual world on a straight footing
In every aspect, even the off-putting.

'Your stomach's got no eyes,' a man once said
Who'd guessed I didn't like how oysters look.
For you I'd stand that saying on its head:
Your eyes have got no stomach. They can brook,
Nay revel in, sights that would strike me dead
And make me queasy even in a book.
I'd like to call it sorcery or knavery
But all too clearly it's a kind of bravery.

[114]

You'd need it, too, if you were here today,
I think I might just mention at this point.
For every sweet young curved hip on display
There squeaks a fearsomely arthritic joint.
Those oiled old hands will never smooth away
The cellulite and wrinkles they anoint,
And many of the bare breasts on parade
Sensationally fail to make the grade.

Squeezed flat and creased like empty toothpaste tubes
Or else inflated to degrees grotesque –
To sum up this array of has-been boobs
The only adjective is Düreresque.
That woman sports a pair of Rubik's cubes.
That woman there could use hers as a desk.
At these exhausted sources of lactation
Words can't convey my lack of fascination.

But back again to literary matters.
One or two critics, I have lately noted,
Are showing signs of going mad as hatters
At hearing you so often praised and quoted.
The strictest of them taciturnly natters
Of how you could well find yourself demoted:
You are too popular and should tread warily.
Also, he says, your lines end arbitrarily.

I always thought *his* ended when the bell
Rang on his Olivetti. Never mind.
Your stanza forms still check out pretty well,
Even if arbitrarily inclined.
They break no rules as far as I can tell.
There are no wasted words that I can find.
In later works your rhythm grows less striking
But that might mean strong rhythm's to my liking.

Speaking of form and rhythm, incidentally,
Two water-nymphs so beautiful I bet
The sight of them would paralyse you mentally
Are playing tennis. It seems I'm the net.
They must be highly privileged parentally:

[115]

Such clear skins and fine bones you only get
When there's a solid family tradition
Of no-expense-spared, well-thought-out nutrition.

Needless to say that with these two the breasts
From every viewpoint seem in A-1 shape,
Though no doubt if it came to tactile tests
There'd be a yielding, as with a ripe grape.
Praise God that they've got those where we've got chests
I muse, while being careful not to gape –
A bald and overweight old coot from Sydney
Who cops a Frog tart's let ball in the kidney.

Now they've pranced off and plunged into a wave
Which warmly fondles them as who would not.
Their gaiety of mood has left mine grave,
Preoccupied with man and his brief lot.
I think of time's hour-glass and bladed stave,
Of how we waste the few days that we've got,
Of how my youth is gone and shan't return.
I must turn over or my back will burn.

I'm writing now in the supine position,
A posture more conducive to high thoughts
Of Culture and the means of its transmission.
From here on in I think you'll find all sorts
Of pundits prophesying the perdition
Awaiting you, complete with boils and warts,
If you should go on proving so appealing
To the unclean, unthinking and unfeeling.

I don't imply, I hasten to assure you,
Your fate's to be a pop star like Kate Bush.
Though seas of spellbound faces stretch before you
The bodies underneath won't pee or push.
I know the more you're buttered up the more you
Will stay as untouched as the Hindu Kush.
Endowed with inspiration of such purity
You'd gladly follow it back to obscurity.

It's obvious that you're a heavyweight:
Your harshest critics can't say otherwise.
Your status would remain inviolate
Though Jeff Nuttall should praise you to the skies.
In that regard you've got it on a plate,
Whence comes the shamrock tinge of certain eyes.
While hitting the jackpot in all essentials
You've managed to hang on to your credentials.

You write intensely *and* you're entertaining.
For those of us less apt to do the first,
Apart from silence there's one course remaining –
Which is to do the second. At the worst
(And when this happens it's no use complaining)
The public clamours to be reimbursed,
But on the whole there's some cause to be proud
If what one writes makes people laugh aloud.

Or so I think when critics in terms drastic
Inform the world my feet are half trochaic.
It seems my scansion's absolutely spastic.
Even my best iambics are spondaic.
The poor fool's sense of rhythm is elastic!
His diction is archaic Aramaic!
As for his rhymes, let's send him back to Kogarah! Hell,
The stuff he drivels isn't even dogarahhell!

It's useless to invoke the semi-vowel
And point out 'bevel' *is* a rhyme for 'Devil'.
The cloth-eared scribes who write prose with a trowel
Will smugly wonder if I'm on the level.
One really might as well throw in the towel.
Fulke Greville's brother was called Neville Greville . . .
No, let the critics stew in their pale juice:
A joke's a joke and it needs no excuse.

Far out on their twin-fin potato chips
The young star surfers sprint to climb astride
A wave as smooth as spit feels on your lips
And when it breaks you see them there inside –

[117]

Born acrobats trained to their fingertips.
Meanwhile here at the thin edge of the tide
A man pretending he's a submarine
To please his children's also in the scene.

A Boudin painted by Tiepolo,
A beige and azure fresco two miles long;
The sky brushed pink, the *sable d'or* aglow,
The plump swell dimpled like a silver gong;
The beach lit by *le ciel*, laved by *les flots*,
An airy glittering shantung sarong,
Unfolds into the south where with a stain
Of Monet nenuphars France turns to Spain.

And though down there the Basques will bomb your car,
Up here they are a people touched with grace.
They know the sweet years only go so far
And life is more than just a pretty face.
However poor and sick and old they are
The sun shines for them, too. They have a place.
A fact which would provoke me to deep thinking
Were not the sun now on the point of sinking.

Clear plum juice simmers in the solar disc.
The soft light off the pale blue water stipples
With gold the green cliff-clothing tamarisk.
The breathing sea sends in its silken ripples.
High on the sea-wall the last odalisque
Looks down with mute approval at her nipples.
La mer, la mer, toujours recommencée.
But that's enough of versing for one day.

I'll get up now and put on thongs and hat.
I'll gather up your books and these few pages.
I'll shake and roll my tatty rattan mat
And up the cliff *trottoir* by easy stages
I'll dawdle with a feeling of that's that –
Great talents may write poems for the ages,
But poetasters with their tongues in fetters
When all else fails at least can still write letters.

To Gore Vidal at Fifty

To Gore Vidal at – how should I commence?
The trick is to strike sparks and still make sense.
To Gore Vidal at fifty – sounds a lot.
Should I be flippant about that, or not?
To Gore Vidal at fifty years of age –
That slights the sprite, though it salutes the sage.
To Gore Vidal at fifty years of youth –
A trifle twee, but closer to the truth,
Since you (I speak in awe, not animosity)
Remain the incarnation of precocity,
A marvellous boy whose man-sized aureola
Still scintillates like fresh-poured Pepsi-Cola
(If I can mention safe from repercussions
The formula that Nixon sold the Russians),
Whose promise is renewed in the fulfilling,
A teenage thrill that goes on being thrilling,
A pledge kept firm with no recourse to perjury
Save incidental, mainly dental, surgery.
And yet you will admit you are no chicken.
Admit? Insist. The Peter Panic-stricken
Might cling to childhood out of self-delusion,
But that or any similar confusion
You've always held in absolute contempt –
The only absolute that you exempt
From your unwearyingly edifying
Assault on mankind's thirst to be undying:
A hope you've never ceased to make a mock of
Or boldly nominate what it's a crock of.
Small wonder you admire that far-off era
The clear lens of your style brings that much nearer,
In which, as Flaubert wrote (and here I quote,
Or, rather, quote what you said Flaubert wrote)
The Gods were dead and Christ was not yet born,
A quick, cold night dividing dusk from dawn,
When man was quite alone, with nothing holier
To call his own than clear-eyed melancholia –

[119]

That penetrating gaze into infinity
Revealing it devoid of all divinity
And transcendental only in its endless
Detachment from our dread of feeling friendless –
A universe which neither plans our grief
Nor pampers us in payment for belief,
But rings its changes utterly unheeding
Though sadist die in bed or saint lie bleeding.
Committed in its course beyond retrieval,
Indifferent to all talk of good and evil,
Unreachable by prayer, untouched by curses,
It tirelessly assembles and disperses,
Created and destroyed and recreated –
Reduced, reprocessed and repristinated;
Its victories defeats, retreats advances,
Its triumphs tragedies, disasters dances,
Its involuted curves of time and distance
All adding up to one fierce, flat insistence –
That its immensities will still be there
When we are not. It simply doesn't *care*.
This is the void that you with the cool grace
Of your prose style help teach us how to face.
This is the pit from which none can escape
Your wit lights up that we might see its shape.
But to convince the world the soul of Marcus
Aurelius must perish with his carcass
Was hard even for him. Most men prefer
To hide their heads in warm sand and not stir.
That public probity, not sexuality,
Is really the foundation of morality –
That justice plays no active part in fate,
Not even when fate leads to Watergate –
That all the prayers and powers of the Kennedys
Buy not one moment's rest from the Eumenides –
That Caesar is not God, nor the good Lord
Someone who walks and talks like Gerald Ford –
With facts like these we find it hard to grapple,
And much prefer to think Eve plucked the apple
Specifically so that redemptive love,
Beamed down on her descendants from above,

Could ease the pangs of her initial blunder
And make us grateful as we knuckle under.
My own view is that mankind would be worse
Than ever should that cloud of dreams disperse,
But your view is the one we're here to praise
For how it penetrates the wishful haze
Which forms when all-too-human self-delusion
Allied with solipsism breeds confusion –
A mist that men call vision as they grope
And choking on it give the name of hope.
So dense a fog will be a long time thinning
So let's call your work thus far a beginning,
And for our own sake wish your life that too –
And, friends before, years more be friends to you.

To Anthony Thwaite at Fifty

Τὸ γὰϱ φοβεῖσθαι τὸν θάνατον λῆϱος πολὺς. πασιν γὰϱ ἡμῖν
τοῦτ᾽ ὀφείλεται παθεῖν.

Aristophanes

Well, Anthony, by now the secret's out
Of what this book is really all about.
The heavyweights have weighed in in your praise
With mighty line and lapidary phrase
Whereby both life and death are shown to be
Imbued with enigmatic majesty.
To celebrate your fifty years of life
The top scribes have been lined up by your wife
To send in something serious, hard-bitten,
Heart-felt and (with a good nib, please) hand-written,
These separate contributions to be sewn
Into a book which for its names alone
Should leave the average *Festschrift* looking bleak
And knocked into the middle of next week,
A synergistic *donativum* that
Should knock all others into a cocked hat.
With such wits to evoke the stern advance
Of Kronos I don't think I stand much chance
Of adding anything in *that* respect.
Monuments of unageing intellect
Have doubtless flooded in, all calculated
To leave you feeling slightly devastated
At how your trim form must perforce disperse
Eventually into the universe,
With random fragments of the quondam you
Attached to wisps of mist and drops of dew.
This leaves me feeling somewhat overparted
And vaguely wondering how to get started,
As well as worried that I've made a gaffe
By using this clapped-out Rapidograph
Instead of the Italic pen or quill
Appropriate to orthographic skill:
The marks that this thing makes look thin and pale
And all in all I feel I'm doomed to fail.

[122]

For deep thoughts and grave words I have no touch.
Qu'allais-je faire dans cette galère? Not much.
But why feign fear at what one does not see?
There might be virtue in necessity.
The grim view, though it must be the initial one,
Needs complementing from the superficial one.
Even to echo Horace's *Eheu*
Fugaces I would have to find it true
And I just don't. I *like* the way the years
Elapse, or anyway I shed few tears.
Perhaps I lack the mental wherewithal
To face the fact that one day night must fall.
Perhaps in smiling at it I'm ignoring it
When what I should be doing is deploring it.
But is one owning up to a soft head
Merely because one's not consumed by dread,
And even finds a strange kind of relief
In hearing, far off, surf roar on that reef
To which, Lucretius says, all things must tend,
Exhausted by the flow of time? We end,
Said Pushkin, to make way for a fresh start
By others: let the new-born give us heart.
'They crowd us from the world,' he wrote, but not
As one who, scared of losing what he's got,
Has really nothing very much to say
Beyond *timor mortis conturbat me* –
He simply found it just, and not just certain,
The play of life should have a final curtain.
(In his case it fell on him like a ton
Of bricks right in the middle of Act One,
Which put the mockers on his flood of song –
But still I think he was more right than wrong.)
'Death joins us to the great majority,'
Droned Edward Young. No quarrel there from me.
'Age', Bacon burbled, 'will not be defied.'
A boring thought that will not be denied,
For fatalism, even as a platitude,
Remains the only reasonable attitude,
While if compounded with inventive verve
Its realism thrills your every nerve,

And has done since the *Iliad* was composed
(In braille – a fact not commonly disclosed).
Some thug on one of Homer's battlefields
Lifts up his voice above the bonging shields
And what he bellows takes away your breath –
And when you get it back you laugh at death.
'The race of men', he half exults, half grieves,
'Is like the generations of the leaves:
They fall in autumn to return in spring.'
A sentiment I find most heartening –
As did, no doubt, the chaps he yelled it to,
And dropped their guard. (And *then* he ran them through.)
The duty you called 'valuing the dust'
In your fine book *Inscriptions* (which I must
Say makes some of our newer bards look tired
Before their time, as well as uninspired)
Remains plain. As that Irish fellow says,
Man is in love and loves what vanishes –
Except he left out one important thing:
A wise man learns to love the vanishing.
Good humour is the mark of those who do,
A virtue highly manifest in you –
Which might sound like an insult to all those
Who think a poet should write about crows
In tones undeviatingly devoid
Of any hint that life's to be enjoyed.
So, Anthony: grow old along with me
And all your friends. The best is yet to be,
Simply because it hasn't happened yet,
And what's to come we never can forget.
It stays sweet till we get to it, at least;
The only wonder that has never ceased –
And that's a fact as certain as my name's
(This line I'll have to pad a bit) Clive James.

Earlier Verse

As I See You

As I see you
Crystals grow
Leaves chime
Roses flow

As I touch you
Tables turn
Towers lean
Witches burn

As I leave you
Lenses shiver
Flags fall
Show's over

The Deep Six

Because the leaves relaxing on the water
Arrange themselves in attitudes of death
Like mannequins who practise languor
I know it must be autumn in the sea.

When the time comes for me to take you there
Through hanging gardens, and all colour trails away
To leave your eyes entirely my secret
And your hair like smoke rising

You will never learn from me about the winter
That will keep us locked at wrist and lips for ever
Like a broken clockwork model of a kiss
When everything is over, where we came from.

Berowra Waters, New South Wales

The seas of the moon are white on white towards evening
Kingfisher strikes head out on the deck for the trees
Veils of tulle are drawn by the dragonflies
The treetops shudder to silence like coins set spinning.

Fireships of cirrus assemble and ride in the west
Tracksuit trousers go on, and a second sweater
Baiting for low-level fish is like writing a letter
To someone whose last name you caught but whose first you
    missed.

The sun goes over the hill with a whole day's flames
The bottles fluoresce going down, like silver spiders
The old astronomers' animals graze the fields of stars
The guttering cirrus drops on the tide to the Sea of Dreams.

The Morning from Cremorne, Sydney Harbour

Someone sets it
Turning again,
Dumps of junk
Jewellery doing
Their slow burn:
Bonbons spill, and a
Rocket rips,
Pops, goes haywire
Inside the head
Of an emerald pit
Some con-man sold
Who's dead, perhaps.

With each night showing
Your share less
You weep for the careless
Day's use:
A play of light
That folds each night
While the milkmen dress.

Con-man, milkman,
Someone wires
The light traps,
Ice fires:
The hail-fall blazing
Trails to dawn
That will take the wraps
Of white glass wool
From the war ships
Coming into their own
Cold steel.

The Lady in Mourning at Camelot

Before the tournament began
She walked abroad in sable sack:
Embattled knights rang hollow when
They tapped each other on the back
And pointed
(Get the one in black)

All plumage is but camouflage
To shapeliness, this lady knew,
And brilliants shame the lips and eyes:
Simplicity, not sadness, so
Became her
(Check. She stole the show)

Four Poems about Porpoises

I

Swallows in leotards
Burrowing holes
Submarine termites
Quicksilver moles

Dazzling galleries
Spiralling aisles
Daydreams in sunlight
Sinking for miles

Hurtling shuttles
Trip up and flee –
Porpoises, weaving
A shot silk sea.

II

In Operation Silent Sails
For submarines at sea last night
The porpoises, on fire with fright
Blew every tube in Fylingdales.

III

I take one look and I know I'm dreaming –
Planing fins and the colour streaming
Boundary layers in the mind.

I take a breath and I'm sure I'm stalling –
Looping blades and the harvest falling:
Grain blown back like a bugle calling
Light brigades along the wind.

I take my ease and I'm scared I'm ageing –
Stunting jets and a war-game raging;
Seas are riddled, undermined.

I take my leave and I know I'm crying
Tears I'll be a lifetime drying,
The tree-house down and the peach tree dying
Home behind.

IV

Porpoises move
Through tunnels of love.

The Banishment

Ma fu' io solo, là dove sofferto
   fu per ciascun di tòrre via Fiorenza,
   colui che la difesi a viso aperto.

Blemishes age
The Arno tonight
The lamps on the bridges
Piledrive light

Kinky bright krisses
Bent new pin
Opal portcullises
Lichees in gin

Bean-rows of breakable
Stakes going in

Chinese brass burnishes.

Pearlshell caskets
Tumble plunder
Soft rose ledges
Give, go under

Bolts of lamé
Fray
Sunder.

If you open slowly
Eyes half crying
That whole flowing
Blurs like dying

Chi'en-Lung
Colours
Run.

Pinking scissors
Choke on velvet:
Cut-throat razors
Rust in claret.

The Crying Need for Snow

It's cold without the softness of a fall
Of snow to give these scenes a common bond
And though, besotted on a viewless rime,
The ducks can do their standing-on-the-pond
Routine that leaves you howling, all in all
We need some snow to hush the whole thing up.

The ducks can do their flatfoot-waterfool
Mad act that leaves you helpless, but in fine
We need their footprints in a higher field
Made pure powder, need their wig-wag line
Of little kites pressed in around the pool:
An afternoon of snow should cover that.

Some crystalline precipitate should throw
Its multifarious weightlessness around
For half a day and paint the whole place out,
Bring back a soft regime to bitter ground:
An instant plebiscite would vote for snow
So overwhelmingly if we could call it now.

An afternoon of snow should cover that
Milk-bottle neck bolt upright in the slime
Fast frozen at the pond's edge, brutal there:
We need to see junk muffled, whitewashed grime,
Lean brittle ice grown comfortably fat,
A world prepared to take our footprints in.

A world prepared to take our footprints in
Needs painting out, needs be a finer field:
So overwhelmingly, if we could call it now,
The fluffy stuff would prime it: it would yield
To lightest step, be webbed and toed and heeled,
Pushed flat, smoothed off, heaped high, pinched anyhow,
Yet be inviolable. Put like that,
Gently, the cold makes sense. Snow links things up.

The Glass Museum

In cabinets no longer clear, each master's exhibit
Of Murano-manufactured glass has the random look,
Chipped and dusty with eclectic descriptive cards,
Of the chemistry set the twelve-year-old abandons,
The test-tubes cracked, the pipette choked solid with dirt:
A work-with-your-hands vocation that never took
And was boxed away near the bottom of the cupboard
Between the clockwork Hornby and the Coldstream Guards.

The supreme exemplars, Ferro, Bigaglia, Radi;
Their prize examples, goblet, bottle and dish;
These classical clearings overgrown in a lifetime
By a jungle of tabular triumphs and tendrilled fish,
Dummy ceramics tricked out with a hand-faked Guardi,
Tubular chandeliers like a mine of serpents:
Age in, age out, the demand was supplied for wonders,
And talent discovered bravura could pay like crime –
To the death of taste and the ruin of common sense.

So the few good things shine on in the junk museum –
A dish with a milk-white helix imprisoned inside,
Miniature polychrome kraters and pocket amphoras
Flambeau-skinned like an oil-slick slimmed by the tide –
While more global-minded than ever the buyers come
By the jet-load lot into Marco Polo to order
Solid glass sharks complete with sucking remoras
Or thigh-high vases certain to sell like a bomb
Whether north of Bering Strait or south of the Border,
As throughout the island the furnaces roar all day
And they crate the stuff in woodswool to barge it across
To Venice which flogs it direct or else ships it away
And must know by now these gains add up to a loss
But goes on steadily selling itself down the river.

In Sydney years ago when my eyes were wider
I would shuffle the midway sawdust at the Easter Show
As the wonder-boy from Murano rolled pipes of glass
In the furnace-glow underneath a sailcloth roof
And expelled his marvellous breath into gleaming spheres
Which abruptly assumed the shape of performing seals,
Silvered inside and no heavier than a moth –
Between the Hall of Mirrors and the Pygmy Princess
Across from the Ferris wheel and the Wall of Death.

The Young Australian Rider,
P. G. Burman

Philip Burman bought an old five hundred
Side-valve BSA for twenty quid.
Unlicensed as they were, both it and him,
He poker-faced ecstatically rode home
In second gear, one of the two that worked,
And everything that subsequently could be done
To make 'her' powerful and bright, he did:
Inside a year she fled beneath the sun
Symphonically enamelled black and plated chrome.

At eighteen years of age he gave up food,
Beer and all but the casual cigarette
To lay his slim apprentice money out
On extra bits like a special needle jet
For a carb the makers never knew about.
Gradually the exhaust note waxed more lewd,
Compression soared, he fitted stiffer springs
To keep the valves from lagging at their duties.
The decibels edged up, the neighbours nearly sued,
Hand over fist that breathed-on bike grew wings
Until her peak lay in the naughty nineties.

Evenings after school I'd bolt my meal
And dive around to his place. In the back
Veranda where he slept and dressed he'd have
Her roaring with her back wheel off the floor
Apocalyptically – the noise killed flies –
Her uncased primary chain a singing blur.
His pet Alsatian hid behind a stack
Of extra wheels, and on the mantelpiece
A balsa Heinkel jiggled through imagined skies.

There was a weekend that we took her out
To Sutherland to sprint the flying mile
Against a mob of Tiger Hundreds. I
Sat wild-eyed and saw his style tell,

Streaming the corners like remembered trails.
They topped him, nearly all of them, but still
They stood around and got the story. 'What
It cost? No bull?' And when we thundered home
I sat the pillion, following his line
Through corners with the drag behind my back
Plucking and fluttering my shirt like sails,
Dreaming his dreams for him of Avus Track,
Of Spa, the Ring, the Isle of Man TT,
The Monza Autodromo and the magic words, Grand Prix.

Two years later, on my spine at Ingleburn
Just after I came back from leave, I thought
Out piece by piece what must have happened.
He was older, and the bike was new: I'd seen
It briefly the year before and heard the things
He planned to do to it. Another BSA,
Still a push-rod job but ohv at least;
One-lung three-fifty. Home-made swinging arm
Both front and rear, a red-hot shaven head,
Light piston, special rings – the heavy stuff.
We lost contact. I kept hearing off and on
How broke he was from racing and improving her.

One Saturday while I practised the Present
With Bayonet Fixed, a thousand entities
In bull-ring splendour of precision blaze
To gladden hearts of all who'd guard our shores,
He banked through Dunlop Corner at Mount Druitt
Leading a pack of AJ7Rs –
All camshaft jobs, but not a patch on him.
A fork collapsed. The bike kicked up and paused,
Her throttle stuck wide open, as he sprawled
With helpless hours to watch her pitch and toss
Like some slow-motion diver on a screen
Before the chain came down across his throat.

I had leave the evening after. Halfway down
The street a neighbour told me at her gate,
And then another neighbour – they were all

Ready and willing, full of homilies
And clucking hindsight. And, I'll give them this,
Of grief, too. He was noisy, but they'd liked him –
'Phil killed himself at Druitt yesterday.'

It's not that I felt nothing. I felt nothingness
Pluck at the armpits of my loose KD's
And balsa models jiggled on their shelves
While soaring roadways hurtled, shoulder high.
I had one thought before I turned away:

The trouble is, with us, we overreach ourselves.

A Line and a Theme from Noam Chomsky*

Furiously sleep; ideas green; colourless
Sweet dreams just lately ain't been had.
Sweat smells like the colour of the jungle.
Things looked bad then. They go on looking bad.

No question Charlie asked for what he got
Below from us, from up there by the jets;
Else their I D-ola G'd've prevailed,
They'd've swum here and stole our TV sets.

We lined 'em up, we knocked 'em down; we smoked.
We finished off what we'd been told to do.
Back Stateside I expected to forget
How heads look when an M16 gets through.

Green nightmares; pillow strangled; sheets mussed up
By day a 'Go' light stops me in my tracks.
Shades don't help: they make the whole *works* green.
A night's sleep is a string of heart attacks.

Furiously sleep; ideas green, colourless
Sweet dreams just lately ain't been had.
That time our gun-ships hit us by mistake,
I was mad then, I mean angry. But this is mad.

* Noam Chomsky gave *furiously sleep ideas green colourless* as an example of a random sequence of words which could have no meaning. It seemed possible that they could, if the context were wide enough, and that their meaning might relate to the Vietnam War, at that time Chomsky's main political concern.

The Outgoing Administration

The Gods have eyes the colour of the sky.
They drink from crystal goblets full of cloud.
They laugh and sing a lot, but not aloud,
Since their appeal is mainly to the eye.

Their games become less hectic with the years,
Their wanton cries too feeble to deceive.
The very sight of them seems keen to leave:
It turns to powder like the salt of tears.

The vivid images are growing soft,
The purple robes are ceasing to wear well.
You see the azure through the muscatel
In all those grapes they've held so long aloft.

To think our children now will never know
How beautiful those creatures used to be,
How much more confident than you and me!
The reason why we had to let them go.

Neither One Thing Nor the Other

Sometimes I think perhaps I'm just obtuse.
Noon yesterday I took a turn through King's.
The crippled physicist came whirring by,
No doubt preoccupied with cosmic things.
I stepped aside. Above us in the sky
A burping biplane shook a glider loose
Whose pilot, swerving sunward, must have felt
As overwhelmingly at liberty
As this man felt pinned down. Was that right, though?
To lie still yet see all might feel more free
Than not to know quite why you're free to go.
The chair hummed off. The glider made no sound.
If I can't fly, why am I not profound?

Le Cirque imaginaire
at Riverside Studios

In 'The Phantom of the Clouds' Apollinaire
Pretended to have gone downstairs to see
The acrobats, and found that when he tried
To drink in what he saw them do, it all
Turned bitter on the tongue. Pink pantaloons
Looked like decaying lungs. The fun was spoiled,
The family act more destitute than when
Picasso painted it. The War was on.
Apollinaire was in it, hence the dudgeon.

Without belittling him, you still might say
He needed horror to dilute delight,
Since childish joy to grown men feels like loss,
If only of childhood. There was a time,
Quite early in *Le Cirque imaginaire*,
When Vicky Chaplin walked on the tight wire
Inverted underneath it, that I thought
I'd just turned five. Her father in his film
The Circus did a stunt like that, but had
To fake it, though with good results. He died
The death in later life, became a bore
About his immortality, which was
No longer under his control. It lives again
When his thin daughter, blessed with Oona's looks,
Draped in sheet silver enters on all fours
High up on four tall stilts that look like six,
A basketballing insect from the depths
Of a benign nightmare.

                    Her husband makes
Surprises happen, just as, long ago,
With something of the same humility,
Her father could. A suitcase full of tricks
Yields up its secrets. Wherein lies the joke:
I mean the joke is that you *see* the way
It works. Except when the huge rabbit,

[144]

Which really *couldn't* be in that red box,
Emerges to remind you that this coy
Parade of diffidence is based on full
Mastery of white magic.

Now the stage
Is full of birds and bouncing animals,
Of which only a few do not excrete.
Silk-slippered on the bare boards pipped with mire,
The happy couple take their curtain calls
And we go back into the world, which has,
No doubt, produced, while we've been gone,
Plenty of stuff to cut this down to size –
Car bombs in day-care centres, *coups d'état*
In countries whose cash crop earns in a year
Less than *Evita* in a so-so week,
A torture farm in California
That takes all major credit cards.

Back in
Reality it needs Apollinaire
(Who went on being right about a war
That cost him half his head) to help retrieve
My reason from the most misleading evening
We spent at the imaginary circus –
Which children shouldn't see without a warning
Things might start looking different in the morning.

Verse Diaries

An Address to the Nation

Dear Britain, Merry Christmas! If I may
Presume on your attention for the space
Of one broadsheet, I'd simply like to say
How pleased I am to see your homely face
Perked up and looking forward to the day
When even the downcast are kissed by grace –
The day a perfect birth is celebrated
And we who are imperfect feel elated.

It's normally the Queen, I'm well aware,
Who takes upon herself the awesome onus
At each year's end of going on the air
And giving us our verbal Christmas bonus.
This year when we switch on she'll still be there,
A crumb of comfort History has thrown us,
Though some, and not the worst, think her the essence
Of suicidal social obsolescence.

But some things can't be said on television
Nor may the Monarch speak of politics.
And thus it is I make the bold decision
In my role as a yokel from the sticks
To grasp the nettle and to court derision
And generally to kick against the pricks
By taking space in this great publication*
Wherewith most humbly to Address the Nation.

Three million out of work and work undone
Because nobody can afford to do it.
A monetarist engine that won't run.
Monetarists who say they always knew it.
A Government which hasn't yet begun
To reap the bitter harvest coming to it.
Next summer if the inner cities burn
Some dolt will say we spend more than we earn.

* *London Review of Books* (December 1981).

[149]

And over there the Loyal Opposition
Is catastrophically split between
Survivors who've long lost their sense of mission
And scolds who say exactly what they mean.
The former are in pitiable condition,
The latter even madder than they're keen.
The old brigade run on the spot like Alice.
The new boys want to storm the Winter Palace.

It's deadlock. Just to get the Tories out
Is no good reason to put Labour in.
One lot's got rabies and the other gout.
Whichever way it goes you just can't win.
The only proper state of mind is doubt
When Parliament sounds like a loony-bin
With each side barracking the other's slogans –
Slogans with whiskers on like Terry Wogan's.

You've reached a turning-point, that much is plain.
It's deeply felt by almost all of you.
The social fabric, if not under strain,
Is further stretched than it's accustomed to.
The body politic cries out in pain
And mere placebos will no longer do,
But just when it seems time to call for surgeons –
Behold! A peaceable solution burgeons!

They style themselves the Social Democrats.
It's their ambition to take centre stage.
On Labour's sinking ship they are called rats
By those who can't swim owing to old age.
Their leaders take an extra size in hats.
They grandly talk of turning a fresh page
In British politics and might well do so –
Or, hitting a new note, croak like Caruso.

The truth is no one can be sure as yet
How this third force will in the long term fare.
Both Labour loyalist and Tory Wet,
Though by their parties driven to despair,

Still say the SDP is a bad bet
And doubt the possibility is there
Of wooing anyone but floating voters –
Exotic types in flannels and straw boaters.

Meanwhile the Liberal half of the alliance
Looks puzzled like a dog wagged by its tail.
The pressure of events dictates compliance
Lest their declining star grow yet more pale.
But offered a back seat some breathe defiance
Preferring to stand on their own and fail.
They too seem to suspect something innately
Unsound about a Johnny come so lately.

What class can it be said to represent?
What ideology does it propose?
Pressed on these points the SDP is meant
To reel back clutching a disjointed nose.
But questions thus put are more eloquent
About the attitudes which they disclose.
The questioner defines his own condition:
A patient who pretends he's a physician.

You British are the only people left
In Europe who are still obsessed by Class.
It sometimes seems you'd rather remain cleft
In twain than see the age-old hoodoo pass.
Without it the West End would be bereft
Of half its drama and of all its farce,
And think of all those books gone down the drain
By Amis, Amis, Bainbridge, Barnes, Bragg, Braine . . .

But artists of all kinds can be excused
For cherishing a stratified society.
Their privilege, which exists to be abused,
Is to lay hold of life in its variety.
Granted they do it well, we are amused
And readily forgive the note of piety
When Brideshead gets paid yet another visit.
It's no more daft than numismatics, is it?

[151]

That stanza was completed in some haste
Because I had to pack, sprint for a plane,
And fly here to this strip of shameless waste
Camped in the midst of the immense inane.
Las Vegas revels in its own bad taste
With neon waterfalls that soak the brain –
A full-tilt celebration of democracy
That makes you think more fondly of theocracy.

And yet despite the uproar of vulgarity,
As always in the US I relax.
Encouraged by the general social parity
Whose class divisions seem no more than cracks.
Notoriously a place that's short on charity
And long on shelters against federal tax,
Vegas breaks hearts and runs bums out of town.
Before you're out, though, you must first be down.

If you can pay, you play. No one excludes you –
A rule of thumb for the whole USA.
There may be a sweet life that still eludes you,
But no codeword you don't know how to say,
No simple accident of birth denudes you
Of dignity. You're free to make your way,
And though one race gets held down by the other
At least they sometimes *talk* to one another.

Americans talk all the time, of course.
They use a lot of words while saying little.
They verbalise until they should be hoarse
Yet somehow don't run short of breath or spittle.
They'll plough on like a saga in Old Norse
And what they say won't mean a jot or tittle:
Semantically it's not much more than static.
It is, however, deeply democratic.

They speak a language everyone can speak,
Which means the tongue-tied aren't left in the cold.
The powerful talk bunkum like the weak,
The timorous talk loudly like the bold.

Even to strangers they all talk a streak.
They drone on while you stand there growing old.
E pluribus unum. Out of the many, one.
It means you'll hear the same mish-mash from anyone.

There's no nuance because there is no rigour,
But in amongst the mush there's often verve.
One can be struck by a demotic vigour,
A heady access of linguistic nerve,
When someone suddenly lets loose a figure
Of speech that like a screwball or a curve
Will swerve around your bat and leave you flailing
Flat-footed, with a feeling that you're failing.

Just such a gift belongs to Melanie,
A neat blonde who deals blackjack at the Sands.
This week she's made a pauper out of me.
The cards that flow like water from her hands
Smoothly entice me into penury,
And yet I could embrace her where she stands
Because her riffles, shuffles, flicks and flutters
Turn pale beside the patter that she utters.

She tells me that I'll never beat the grind
Unless I bet big with the house's money
While I'm ahead. 'But don't pay me no mind.
You got a special style that's all yours, honey.'
In this light you can't tell her face is lined.
There was a day she was a Playboy Bunny,
And when it's time to take up a new trade
You can be sure that she won't be afraid.

Having your health bills paid from womb to tomb
Strikes Melanie as organised servility.
She claims she'd scream from lack of elbow room.
She cherishes her own adaptability.
She's certain that one welfare cheque spells doom
For any spark of spiritual agility.
She sounds, in other words, like Margaret Thatcher –
Though words are just where Thatcher couldn't match her.

[153]

It's easy for the Yanks to preach self-help:
There's so much protein they can help themselves.
In Britain we'd be feeding children kelp
And watching them grow up the size of elves
Were we to heed the age-old Tory yelp
That's heard when the tinned goods on the shop shelves
Are priced so as those people can afford them
Who'll only eat them when they ought to hoard them.

Our film on gambling is completely shot
So back we fly to where it's cold and poor.
There it was hot and rich but here it's not.
Yes, here now feels less nice than there before.
There is a lot that Britain has not got –
A fact it takes some effort to ignore.
(I fear this stanza's a bit elementary:
I'm shattered by the impact of re-entry.)

A news flash. In the latest by-election
The Liberal William Pitt has won the seat.
His personal appeal defies detection.
At previous attempts he met defeat.
Clearly it is the SDP connection
Which has supplied the upsurge of white heat
That melts the Tory vote to a minority
And Labour's to abject inferiority.

This Pitt falls far short of so grand a name.
Long in the beard, he's less so in the legs.
He lacks the stature for his sudden fame.
It's plain that of the Pitts he is the dregs,
And yet he is a Titan all the same.
The great name lives again as sure as eggs:
For Mr Steel, Pitt *minimus* will function
To bless and sanctify the new conjunction.

With no more murmurs in the Liberal ranks
In Labour's there is total consternation.
If Michael Foot tore out his hair in hanks
He could not look more prone to perturbation.

[154]

The right wing loudly calls the left wing cranks
And no one stays calm in the altercation
Except for Tony Benn, who sucks contentedly
On his prop pipe and stares ahead dementedly.

What does he see there in the depths of space?
Still half-defined, it sets his large heart beating.
The vision clarifies and lights his face.
He sees some vast canteen in which a meeting
Of Britain's work-force endlessly takes place
And no one minds the lack of central heating.
What lifts their spirits? Why are they ecstatic?
Because their chairman is so charismatic!

No, Destiny demands he try again
To wrest the Party from the Right's dead grip.
He stems from a long line of working men.
His fellow workers need his leadership.
Lord Stansgate walks the earth as Tony Benn.
He comes to cleanse the temple with his whip.
They've crucified him once. It felt quite nice.
No reason why it shouldn't happen twice . . .

Healey, meanwhile, turns beetroot red with rage,
His jowls so vibrant he can hardly speak.
The right ideas, the right looks, the right age –
And yet his place is filled by an antique,
While fools ensure a once-proud heritage
Goes down a tube that comes out up the creek.
But he and Hattersley must grin and bear it:
The cap Benn gives them fits. They have to wear it.

The Labour Right's lip-service to Clause 4
Now stands revealed as outright atheism.
They simply don't believe it any more,
Hence the exultant rancour of the schism.
The heretics have nine points of the law.
The creed they preach is Fundamentalism.
They say the Right is Socialist no longer.
They say the truth, and so they must grow stronger.

But purified or not, the Labour cause
Within our time could dwindle to a rump.
Not for the sake of some outdated clause:
It's just that people tend to get the hump
When told too often that Behind Closed Doors
Ten million union votes cast in one lump
By some strange means have all made the same choice.
Whatever happened to the human voice?

The Tory version of it now seems camper
Than ever. Thatcher's condescending whine
Was always guaranteed to put a damper
On anybody's urge to rise and shine.
She made you want to pack a wicker hamper
And have a picnic down a disused mine,
But still the odd factotum like Jim Prior
At least seemed relatively a live wire.

Now Prior's gone and in comes a new broom
Named Twitchit. Rabbit? Sorry, I mean Hobbit.
His eyes like lasers penetrate the gloom.
He takes the nation's pulse like William Cobbett.
He paces, ponders, clears his throat of rheum
And in due course gives forth this juicy gobbet:
We must work harder. That's what we must do.
(No need to add that by 'we' he means you.)

That's the Employment Secretary's plan
For getting us out of our present mess.
One wonders if he's really the right man.
He should be tagging wildlife in Loch Ness.
The CBI are back where they began,
Frantically making signals of distress.
They said they wanted to be lean and mean
And now they are, and now they're not so keen.

Inflation slows but industry slows faster
And British Leyland might grind to a halt.
The strike looms like a nuclear disaster
Except no expertise can trace the fault.

The management's run out of sticking plaster.
The Cabinet might perform a somersault
Or else stand firm where previously it wouldn't,
Or would have done but as things stood it couldn't.

The policy said No Help For Lame Ducks.
Reality said big lame ducks must eat.
A lame duck that makes half our cars and trucks
Could put a million people on the street.
For such a bird the treatment is de luxe
Lest it should trip over those awkward feet.
Hence the webbed boots and plastic knee-protector
Paid for by cutting back the public sector.

Leaving the Mini Metros to their fate
I pack my bag again and take the air,
Progressing south-east at a dizzy rate
Until I look down and see Sydney there.
The Harbour Bridge looks like a paperweight,
The Opera House like fractured Tupperware.
It all shines like quicksilver in the dawn.
Cloud-cuckoo-land. The land where I was born.

Here when the young are forced to take the dole
It just means they spend more time at the beach.
Thinkers bemoan the country's lack of soul
While still contriving to own three cars each.
You scoop wealth up like opals from a hole.
All you can dream of is within arm's reach,
And no one mugs you, kidnaps you or taunts you –
Though sometimes you might find your conscience haunts you.

As our world goes this is an unreal land,
A paradise devoid of modern menaces,
A land where Eve and Adam hand in hand
Star in a rewrite of the book of Genesis.
Recumbent Adam gets his forehead fanned
While wooing Eve in verse like C. J. Dennis's.
They won't be asked to leave. They're set for ever.
They've got the freehold of the Never-Never.

[157]

I'm here to plug my book from town to town.
All day I'm either in the air or on it.
The first time I wrote that last stanza down
It came out three lines longer than a sonnet.
I'm having trouble telling verb from noun.
Quid verbis opus est? A plague upon it.
But after all it's just the flesh that's tired.
The spirit's willing, not to say inspired.

Inspired above all by the piercing twang
Of Austral voices flagrantly projected,
Astringent as the antiseptic tang
Of iodine upon the place infected.
It might not be the song the sirens sang.
You might wish that your ears were disconnected,
But still you must admit there's something stimulating
In how they have no notion of dissimulating.

They may lack subtlety who have no guile.
They often – it's their own word for it – whinge.
The open freckled face they call the dial
With injured pride adopts a purple tinge.
Often they bristle when they ought to smile,
But what you never see them do is cringe.
Would-be sophisticate or brute barbarian,
Your Aussie is a true egalitarian.

But now the demon bowler Dennis Lillee
By his behaviour starts a frightful barney.
Too much success too young has made him silly.
He kicks the shin of a small Pakistani.
Here and in Britain the Press willy-nilly
Combines to sing a chorus from *Ernani*.
All are agreed that such obtuse aggression
Denotes the opposite of self-possession.

Perhaps they're right. No people should be praised
For confidence when they are so well fed.
Needless to say I'm suitably amazed
At how my native land has gone ahead,

[158]

But when one's had one's turn at looking dazed
Reluctantly it also must be said
That anywhere so prodigally blessed
Is ultimately short of interest.

Australia's cities remain safe and clean,
The public telephones unvandalised.
Like free advertisements the beach-girls preen
In costumes overstressed and undersized.
Once more as I take off from Tullamarine
I feel to leave all this is ill-advised,
But also, floating over the Dead Heart,
Feel somehow not unhappy to depart.

Down there in that hot ocean of red rock
There is no history, only geography.
Some ethnic dance-group may attempt to shock
With semi-nude formation choreography,
But basically this place has stopped the clock,
Made time a tableau like high-speed photography.
It's only at the fertile utmost fringes
The age we're living in even impinges.

Dante's Ulysses told his trembling crew
They should not stay like beasts where life was easy,
And Baudelaire, who sailed to find the new,
Best recognised it when it made him queasy.
Australians with a thirst for derring-do
Find modern Britain challengingly sleazy –
It's chill, dank, broke, pale, dirty, constipated,
But also tough, real, quirky, complicated.

Heathrow at dawn is cloud down to the ground,
Black taxis queue as if for the bereaved.
The body of a child has just been found.
It seems that British Leyland is reprieved.
One Aussie dollar buys almost a pound.
Welcome to Britain. Why am I relieved?
Because although life here is far less pleasant
Nevertheless it happens in the present.

Foot now at last and probably too late
Tells Benn to either belt up or get lost,
While Thatcher at an ever-quickening rate –
As if there were some profit in the cost –
Unbolts large pieces of the Welfare State
Which lying in the rain rust where they're tossed.
Good people in both parties look hag-ridden.
Small anguished cries come to their lips unbidden.

The Crosby by-election, shriek the polls,
Must go to Shirley Williams by a cable.
Should that occur the toiling Fleet Street trolls
Will find her shapelier than Betty Grable,
While making sure a solemn tocsin tolls
To tell Roy Jenkins he is not Clark Gable.
About the top spot there'll be much palaver
As some fans cry *bravo*! and others *brava*!

Someone will have to lead the SDP.
Ten Downing Street won't sleep a whole committee.
In all good time a choice there'll have to be
But making it too soon would be a pity,
Lest we, bombarded by publicity,
Lose touch with what should be the nitty-gritty –
That polite knock on the large door at the centre
Outside which common reason waits to enter.

Perhaps by now it's been too long outside,
Hat in one hand, the other with raw knuckles.
Perhaps by now it's gaunt and hollow-eyed,
Wearing a powdered wig and shoes with buckles.
Perhaps it will take one unsteady stride
Before dissolving into drunken chuckles,
But what most of us hope we will be seeing
Is just a reasonable human being.

The secret of the so-called common touch
Resides in its appeal to common sense.
Though simply to talk straight might not seem much
The consequences could just be immense.

[160]

Now that the country's choking in the clutch
Of toxic verbal fog at its most dense,
Merely to speak in terms that do not slight us
Might almost be enough to reunite us.

Which must be done *before* the long slow task
Of getting well again is undertaken.
The patient's lying there in a gauze mask,
Fed through a vein and feeling Godforsaken.
He'll do the twenty press-ups that you ask
But first his will to live must reawaken.
He must hear in your voice the note of sanity
Struck by acknowledgment of shared humanity.

As long as the Alliance can talk sanely
It will not so much matter for the nonce
That when it moves it is a bit ungainly
And stumbles off six different ways at once.
Would-be hard-bitten critics snipe inanely,
There's mockery from every hack and dunce,
But for most people that uncertain feeling
Is just what makes the new lot so appealing.

By now the big ideas have all been tried,
Become bad jokes we have grown sick of hearing.
The economic rough-stuff on one side,
The other's dreams of social engineering,
Render the average punter gratified
That honest doubt at last is reappearing.
At least this bunch don't spout like know-it-alls
The usual load of patronising balls.

Ideally they should stay unencumbered
With whopping programmes that they can't enforce.
It's still the classic way of getting lumbered.
The cart is meant to be *behind* the horse.
There is no need to feel our days are numbered,
Only to trace the power to its source:
The people's good will is what drives the nation
And holds the secret of regeneration.

Ms Williams wins. This time she caught the train.
But BL's Longbridge plant is still on strike.
From Ireland comes the daily scream of pain.
It's still the same old story if you like.
The deep-ingrained uncertainties remain.
The Way Ahead's a hell of a long hike.
You've not a jot in common but the weather.
The rain's the only thing you're in together.

The rain, the sleet and soon, no doubt, the snow.
Through autumn into winter I have scribbled
This crackerbarrel tract at which I know
The expert commentators will wax ribald.
This is a complex subject, they will crow,
A mountain range at which a mouse has nibbled –
But I still think the British within reason
Have reason to be glad this festive season.

Poem of the Year

(1982)

To C. L. Perowne
and the Downhill Badger

I

The old year ends with Cambridge under snow.
The world in winter like the moon in spring
Unyieldingly gives off a grey-blue glow.
An icy laminate caps everything.
Christmas looks merry if you wish it so.
One strives to hark the Herald Angels sing,
But at each brief hiatus in the feast
A bitter wind howls sadly from the east.

In Poland now the only Santa Claus
Is General Jaruzelski looking grim.
With Solidarity a brave lost cause
There is no father figure except him.
His overall demeanour gives one pause.
Nor are peace prospects really made less dim
By Ronald Reagan recommending firm
Measures that make his NATO allies squirm.

Snow falls again. The atmosphere turns white.
The airfields of East Anglia are socked in.
The atom bombers will not fly tonight.
Tonight the Third World War will not begin.
There's so much concentrated heat and light
Stored around here that if they pulled the pin
The British Isles would be volatilised.
Even the dons would be a bit surprised.

One theory says the Polish Army acted
Only to stop the Russians doing worse.
So clumsily to have a tooth extracted
By family friends calls forth a garbled curse,
But left too long the fang will get impacted
And you won't like the dentist or his nurse.
At least – the pun's not just weak but emetic –
Get the job done with *local* anaesthetic.

Such reasoning is comfortable like us
But soon there are dark rumours to belie it.
The fact the coup has led to far more fuss

Than they say, you can tell when they deny it.
Here in the West we have much to discuss
Beyond the danger to a healthy diet.
You like the thin mints? Try the orange sticks.
Has anybody seen the walnut picks?

Most of the Poles have not got much to eat.
Their democratic leaders have still less.
A cold and cruel and long-drawn-out defeat
Must be the price they pay for small success.
They bucked a system that they could not beat
Which reasserts itself through their distress.
White flakes may decorate the searchlight beams –
The barbed wire is exactly what it seems.

Those men and women braver than the brave
Penned in the open air are telling you
It's better to risk death than be a slave –
Something you thought that you already knew.
And yet to stick together till the grave –
Could we do that if that's what it came to?
One's rather glad one's not cast as a hero
Out there tonight at twenty below zero.

The turkey carcass and Brazil-nut shells
And mandarin rinds fill the pedal bin.
The ice-rimmed church and college chapel bells
Stiffly combine to call the New Year in.
The snow melts and in London the Thames swells
As once the lake lapped Tantalus's chin,
But as I leave the usual filthy train
I guess that the embankments took the strain,

Or else my book-lined eyrie near St Paul's
Would look down on a city rather like
Venice or Amsterdam plus waterfalls
Cascading over many a broken dike.
There'd be ducks nesting in the choir stalls
Of Clement Dane's, and people would catch pike
(With suitably refined outbursts of joy)
From windows at the back of the Savoy.

[168]

But there is nothing underfoot save slush
Compounded from crushed ice, old snow and dirt.
Your wellies slurp and gurgle in the mush.
Spat by a taxi wheel the stuff can spurt
Up from the street in one exultant gush
To inundate you where you stand inert.
The cars and buses churn the rhubarb slurry
Until it darkens into cold beef curry.

Schmidt goes to Washington and tells the Yanks
That while his Germany might still be Jerry
The Russians are not Tom and have large tanks
Whose side-effects it can take weeks to bury.
Therefore he is reluctant to give thanks
For Reagan's speeches, which to him seem very
Naive, as if designed to aggravate
The blind intransigence they castigate.

Congress is humbled by Schmidt's eloquence
Which makes the President sound like an actor
Who reads a script well but is slightly dense
If not as crass as Carter on his tractor.
The Chancellor's impact has been immense.
Intelligence emerges as a factor
In statesmanship and might well start a fashion
Of saying things with point and not just passion.

But whether he is right is hard to judge.
Meanwhile the snow which only last week went
Comes back as if it bore a lasting grudge
And whites the country out from Wales to Kent.
On the M4 the lorries do not budge.
The usual helicopters have been sent
To find the troops last seen the day before
Searching for lost bird-watchers on Broadmoor.

In no time the whole country's ten feet deep:
Landscapes by Breughel, cityscapes by Lowry.
They're using sonar gear to find the sheep.
All Europeans get this as a dowry

But after twenty years I still could weep,
Feeling more foreign to it than a Maori.
I'm half delighted and I'm half disdainful –
It looks so lovely and it feels so painful.

Roy Jenkins will be standing at Hillhead
In Glasgow. The world wonders: is this wise?
Lose Warrington and it's a watershed:
Defeat there was a victory in disguise.
But this time if he doesn't win he's dead
With all his party sharing his demise.
The SDP, awed by its own audacity,
Strikes postures of unflappable sagacity.

But more of that – much more, no doubt – anon.
Meanwhile Mark Thatcher's managed to get lost
Somewhere in Africa. The hunt is on.
Airborne armadas at tremendous cost
Search all directions where he might have gone.
One tends to find one's fingers slightly crossed.
The days go by and soon it's not a joke.
He's even talked of as a nice young bloke.

Since he in fact is something of a prat
This sudden fondness constitutes a proof
The British heart still beats though lagged with fat.
His mother weeps who once was so aloof
But few there are who take delight in that.
Many who think her son a cocksure goof
And wish her and her politics in hell
Nevertheless in this case wish her well.

The boy is found and instantly reverts
To his accustomed status, that of jerk.
The next blow to the nation really hurts.
ASLEF the footplate union will stop work.
The papers tell us we'll all lose our shirts
Because train-drivers can't forgo a perk.
The sum of Fleet Street's pitiless analysis
Presages chaos, followed by paralysis.

If Fleet Street takes so unified a vew
We can be sure the truth must lie elsewhere.
The first train strike of 1982
Inspires more irritation than despair.
Unmotivated locos are not new.
What's fearsome is when planes fall from the air.
In Washington one does. Down on the bed
Of the ice-locked Potomac sit the dead.

The whole world tuning in through television
For once sees human nature at its best.
A man who might have lived makes the decision
To stay and try to save some of the rest.
Were this a movie, think of the derision
With which we'd greet such an absurd *beau geste*.
On that small screen the big hole in the ice
Frames the reality of sacrifice.

II

The feeling that there's grandeur in mankind
Is soon dispelled by fresh cause for lament.
A rapist is not jailed but merely fined
Because, it seems, the girl was 'negligent'.
Perhaps the judge has gone out of his mind,
Unless it's him that's straight and us that's bent.
He's set the price for screwing a hitch-hiker:
Two grand. Just toss her out if you don't like her.

Fleet Street, which always disapproved of rape
Despite provoking hot lust on page three,
This time gets on its high horse and goes ape.
In Scotland several men have been set free
Because the woman is in such bad shape
She can't be called on to give testimony.
The man in charge says it's an awkward case.
He's got a point, but no one likes his face.

So Nicky Fairbairn now gets pulled apart
Both in the House and by the public prints.
I must confess I'm not touched to the heart.

That 'style' of his has always made me wince.
I've never liked his haircut for a start,
Nor the sharp trews in which he's wont to mince.
His *Who's Who* entry puts the lid on it:
He has the hide to call himself a Wit.

That title's one which nobody can claim.
You have to wait for others to bestow it.
Not even Oscar Wilde assumed the name,
Who called himself both genius and poet.
That he was self-appointed to his fame –
A true wit wouldn't hint it, much less crow it.
Poor knackered Nicky thinks he's Alan Coren:
He's just a wee laird with a twitching sporran.

And yet it's wise to give conceit expression –
Within the limits set by the absurd.
A boast might be self-serving like Confession
But similarly festers if unheard.
Much meekness stands revealed as self-obsession
When self finds a release too long deferred.
Beware the kind of people who don't flower
Until their shrivelled roots taste fame and power.

Take Henry Kissinger as an example.
The man personifies megalomania.
He's back in action with another sample
Of foreign policy from Ruritania.
On Poland Reagan's harsh words have been ample
But Henry hankers after something zanier.
Leave it to me, he seems to be implying,
And Russian fur will pretty soon be flying.

Suslov checks out. Unless he died of fright
At Henry's rhetoric, it's just old age
That now removes Stalin's last acolyte
And faithful killer gently from the stage.
The mental stature of potato blight
Left him unchallenged as the Party sage:
The perfect man to make sure Ideology
Maintained its power to torture by tautology.

They bury Suslov in the Kremlin wall:
A tribute to his cranial rigidity.
Propped up like that the bricks will never fall.
Meanwhile the intellectual aridity
He helped create still casts its stifling pall:
A dry red dust of cynical stupidity
Ensures the last trace of imagination
Is wept away in hot tears of frustration.

Frustration, but the trains do run on time –
Mainly because the drivers must keep driving
Since any form of strike would be a crime.
No doubt there are time-honoured forms of skiving.
Perhaps their trains, like ours, are sprayed with grime
Before they leave and once more on arriving.
They do, however, go. Without delay.
And what is more they do so every day.

Ours at the moment run five days a week
Or four days, subject to negotiation.
It might be three days even as I speak:
I've lost track of the inverse escalation.
The union leaders talk their usual Greek.
The matter must not go to arbitration.
The strike must bite. The strike days must be staggered.
Sir Peter Parker still smiles but looks haggard.

Sir Peter Parker picked a pickled peck
Of pepper when he took on British Rail.
With every kind of triumph at his beck
And call, perhaps he felt the need to fail.
His chance of saving something from the wreck
Equals his chance to find the Holy Grail.
You never know, though. He and Sidney Weighell
Might possibly cook up some sort of deighell.

If Buckton's ASLEF joined Weighell's NUR
Then BR's board plus ACAS minus VAT . . .
We might as well give up and go by car
Or coach, or on foot if it comes to that.

[173]

Some say the train lines should be paved with tar,
Which no doubt counts as talking through your hat,
But if it's true what's needed most is cash
Then stand aside and watch out for the crash.

It's no time to owe money at the bank,
A fact now underlined by Freddie Laker –
Although in part he has the banks to thank
His airline's laid out for the undertaker.
It seems they lent him dough as if they drank
Their lunch directly from the cocktail shaker,
But now the plugs are pulled and in mid-flight
His planes turn back as he gives up the fight.

Disconsolate the DC10s come home
To Gatwick, where in time someone will buy them.
An airliner is not a garden gnome.
They can't just sit there. Somebody will fly them.
Defeated legions coming home to Rome
Would choose new emperors and deify them,
But Freddie, though his hearty laugh rings hollow,
Is not an act just anyone can follow.

Sir Freddie, Thatcher's knight with shining wings,
Her favourite Private Sector buccaneer,
Seems to have made rather a mess of things.
Is this collapse the end of his career?
His air of loosely buckled swash still clings.
The cut-price flying public holds him dear.
They send pound notes to keep Skytrain in motion –
Straws in the wind although drops in the ocean.

Here's proof the people value enterprise
And overlook, in those they think have got it,
A Rolls like Freddie's of excessive size,
A house so big an astronaut could spot it.
Whatever shibboleth might galvanise
The public, public ownership is not it.
Despite the very real risk of fatalities
People identify with personalities.

Just when Sir Freddie masticates the dust
The civil servants get their indexed pensions.
Not only Thatcher fans express disgust
At this exposé of the inner tensions
Between what she would like to do and must.
It is an awkward fact she seldom mentions:
The spread she said she'd end of public spending
Increases, and the increase is unending.

She can't trim bureaucratic overmanning.
She cuts the social services instead.
You needn't be as wise as Pitt or Canning
To see how malnutrition lies ahead.
Conversely, Labour's universal planning
Is just the cure to leave the patient dead.
The Alliance must win if it has the nerve to.
At this rate if they don't they don't deserve to.

III

A thought to bear in mind as we now watch
The Labour Party tear at its own guts.
The Peace of Bishop's Stortford's a hotch-potch
Which to place faith in you must first be nuts.
With moulting mane Foot still attempts to scotch
All doubts by well-placed ha-has and tut-tuts,
But while he waffles wanly about unity
The toughs build up their beachhead with impunity.

The Peace of Bishop's Stortford lulls the press
Which now says it's the SDP that's split.
The lead of the Alliance has grown less,
The tabloids chortle, champing at the bit.
Alliance policies are in a mess
And all in all this new lot aren't quite it.
On Tebbit's union bill they show dissension –
Clear indication of internal tension.

[175]

De Lorean the glamour-puss tycoon
Whose gull-wing car is built with our tax money
Might lay at least a gull-sized egg quite soon.
He's suave and clever and his wife's a honey.
For Northern Ireland he has been a boon.
But still and all there's something slightly funny . . .
Or maybe I just find the car too dull,
Attractive only to another gull.

At any rate, the books are with Jim Prior,
Who must decide if we should drop De Lorean
And cut the loss or raise the ante higher.
De Lorean's first name should have been Dorian:
That ageless face of the *Playboy* high-flyer
Is decomposing like an ancient saurian.
I think he's guilty mainly of wild dreams
And now he sees them cracking at the seams.

Prior pronounces. Not another penny
Of public funds. De Lorean must raise
The cash himself. Has he himself got any?
His blink-rate slows to a stunned mackerel glaze.
No doubt he has some rich friends but how many?
He has to find the moola in two days.
Meanwhile the bootlace leeches of Fleet Street
Come sucking up in search of easy meat.

De Lorean finds every well is dry
And Prior duly puts in the Receiver,
Who luckily is not just the one guy
Since lately he's been working like a beaver.
Times Newspapers might be the next to die,
Tossing and turning with the self-same fever.
A mighty panic's on to kill things off.
They're giving the last rites at the first cough.

To think the SDP is on the wane –
While Labour's somehow on the comeback trail –
Unless I am a Dutchman is insane.
I don't say the Alliance cannot fail.

I just say that they cannot fail to gain
If Labour puts itself beyond the pale
By dosing its venereal infection
With Valium until the next election.

The bubble's burst already. It's revealed
The Militants have plans by which the fate
Of all non-Marxist MPs would be sealed
And power would go leftward on a plate.
All bets are off and it's a battlefield.
Poor Foot is in a terrifying state,
While Benn's grin says with fathomless hypocrisy
That's what you get for holding down Democracy.

The Tendency's great plot, is it a fact?
It could be fake like the Zinoviev letter.
There's something phoney about this whole act.
When people plot red plots don't they plot better?
They can't be nincompoops as *well* as cracked.
You'd get a better plot from a red setter.
They should have signed it with the mark of Zorro.
Perhaps *The Times* will tell us all, tomorrow.

I go to buy my paper the next day
Feeling that every *Times* may be my last,
And meet Neil Kinnock making a *tournée*
Of St Paul's Yard. He's gleefully aghast
At the Red Plot. 'You'd think the CIA
Had written it!' But it was moved and passed
And signed, sealed and delivered through the post
By these dumb-clucks. They've served themselves on toast.

Brave Kinnock thinks his cause will by this blunder
Be further armoured in defence of sanity.
I'd hate to see good men like him go under:
So much charm rarely has so little vanity.
But why else is his party torn asunder
If not because the measure of humanity
He represents is deemed not just outdated
But doomed to be hacked down and extirpated?

For Benn's and Scargill's Labour I won't vote.
For Kinnock's I would think it churlish not to.
Foot knows most voters are like me and float
And that to win them he has simply got to
Keep down the ranters who get people's goat.
He must do something but does not know what to.
Frank Hooley booted out at Sheffield Heeley
And now Fred Mulley too! It's too much, really.

Foot's shuffling feet should be in carpet slippers
But clearly Kinnock remains loyal still.
As he and his nice wife and their two nippers
Pursue their half-term hike down Ludgate Hill,
Threading between the tourists and day-trippers,
They seem to incarnate the People's Will.
I only wish that such a thing existed
And like a cherished building could be listed.

As Amersham achieves Privatisation
And sells the way hot cakes do when dirt cheap
We realise with a sickening sensation,
As of a skier on a slope too steep,
That if the soundest firms owned by the nation
Are flogged, the duds are all we'll get to keep –
And when the auction ends they'll sell the hammer.
We're heading downhill faster than Franz Klammer.

On that one deal the public's out of pocket
Some umpteen million quid or thereabouts.
Thatcher gives everyone concerned a rocket
But *re* her policy betrays no doubts.
Around her neck she wears a heart-shaped locket
In which lie curled some undernourished sprouts
Of Milton Friedman's hair plucked from his head
Or elsewhere during hectic nights in bed.

I speak in metaphor, needless to say:
Milton and Maggie you could not call lovers
Save in the strictly intellectual way
By which they sleep beneath the same warm covers

And wake up side by side to face the day
Throbbing in concert like a pair of plovers –
Though Milty while he shaves sometimes talks tough
And tells her she's not being rough *enough*.

Monetarism as an orthodoxy
Is lethal preached by one like the PM,
Precisely *because* she's got so much moxie.
She burns deep like the hard flame from a gem,
Sticks to her guns like glutinous epoxy,
And views the dole queues others would condemn
As growing proof that cutting out dead wood
Can in the long run only lead to good.

No need to say those millions on the dole
Are there because the Government decrees it.
The contrary idea is a live coal,
A notion so dire that the mind can't seize it.
Suppose that unemployment on the whole
Would be the same no matter what . . . Stop! Cheese it!
Better believe that Maggie acts from malice,
Childishly spiteful like JR in *Dallas*.

An aircraft hijacked in Dar es Salaam
Arrives at Stansted full of Tanzanians.
The Immigration officers keep calm
Almost as if these folk were Europeans.
One wouldn't want to see them come to harm.
Stansted's a long way north of New Orleans.
But dash it all, eh what! What a kerfuffle
Just to sort out some minor tribal scuffle!

It seems these hijack chappies hate Nyerere
And think that Stansted's the best place to say it.
The SAS are on tap looking scary,
A mighty strong card if we have to play it.
As hijacks go, though, this one's airy-fairy.
The price they ask is vague and kind words pay it.
Believing that their cause is understood
They throw down weapons mostly carved from wood.

A mess on our own doorstep's thus averted.
What started it we fail to comprehend.
Once more we in the plush West have asserted
Our will that awkwardness must have an end.
And yet it's possible that we've just flirted
With some great hurt no words of ours can mend,
In which we might well once have had a hand –
A homing chicken coming in to land.

IV

Speaking of which, one fears that Mr Thorpe
Will not reign long as Amnesty's new chief.
Placed under stress he has been known to warp,
As David Astor points out with some grief.
I must say that Thorpe's nerve gives cause to gawp.
A decent silence should not be so brief.
One does feel he might wear more sober togs
And do things quietly in aid of dogs.

Marcus Aurelius said there's an age
Beyond which we should scorn the public eye,
Put down our seals of office, quit the stage,
Settle our business and prepare to die.
No one denies the Emperor was a sage:
His precepts, though, we nowadays defy.
Old Brezhnev, for example, will stay there
As long as there's enough dye for his hair.

Perhaps he's dead already and controlled
Remotely by a powerful transmitter.
Another waxwork poured in the same mould
Might stir up protest or at least a titter.
His chassis, valves and circuits have grown old.
The struggle to replace them could be bitter.
At checking-out time for the ape-faced gremlin
Try to avoid the front desk of the Kremlin.

But just as I write this the rumour's rife
That Brezhnev's had it and the fight is on
For who'll be next to taste immortal life

[180]

As General Secretary when he's gone.
Silent arrests and kindred signs of strife
Compose the usual deaf-mute telethon.
One man scores points for standing near another
But drops out when denounced by his own mother.

How droll these thugs would be if not so sad,
Watching their backs and also the main chance.
Most aren't insane or even mildly mad.
Each owns a blue suit with two pairs of pants.
By now they think Marxism was a fad
But still they hold that men should live like ants
While they themselves adorn the doll museum
Standing on top of Lenin's mausoleum.

Blue-jawed top dogs of the *Nomenklatura*
They loom while squads of workers toting spanners
Come stomping by like Nazis past the Führer
Except the signs are different on the banners.
The *idée fixe* is still that a bravura
Performance turns this comedy of manners
Into some species of impressive drama
Instead of just a childish diorama.

According to the *Sunday Times*, Pat Wall,
Prospective Labour MP (Militant),
Has risen on hirsute hind legs to bawl
A vintage load of Jacobinist cant,
Insisting that the Monarch, Lords and all
Such privileged figures strangely yet extant,
Must forthwith holus-bolus be abolished
Or strictly speaking physically demolished.

Wild Wall includes the judges in his fury,
Which indicates that when he comes to power
As well as MP he'll be judge and jury –
A prospect at which even saints might cower.
The Party handles him as Madame Curie
Handled her radium hour after hour,
Unmindful that the steady radiation
In her own blood and bones worked devastation.

But now South Africa becomes the focus
Of every cricket lover's expert gaze,
While those who think the great game hocus-pocus,
A ritual rain-dance that goes on for days
Until the grey clouds open up and soak us,
This time can only look on in amaze
As British cricketers receive abuse
For being not just tiresome but obtuse.

Boycott, we hear, should live up to his name,
And not be one by whom sanctions are busted.
He and his mates of almost equal fame
Could well prove to have been falsely entrusted
With their credentials in the holy game.
Students of sport pronounce themselves disgusted
Since segregated cricket, in a sense,
Is like denying blacks the sacraments.

Apartheid has not much to recommend it.
What else can it engender except hate?
One day the blacks will find a way to end it
Their masters will not spot until too late.
Meanwhile the sole good reason to defend it
Somebody should be brave enough to state:
With all of the appropriate delights
Top-level cricket is reserved for whites.

You must be white to wear the proper cap
And have a drink while you watch Boycott bat
And during lunch go down and meet the chap
And slap him on the back and have a chat
And go back up and take a little nap
And finally he's run out and that's that.
Yes, that was Boycott's finest innings yet:
Those fifteen runs that took three days to get.

Boycott was born to give the Wisden bores
The perfect subject for their lucubrations.
He is the average oaf whose average scores
Are averaged out in their long computations,

Reducing you to helpless yawns and snores.
Like small boys spotting trains in railway stations,
They fall into the deep trance of the mystic
Merely by contemplating some statistic.

The Thunderer survives. To celebrate
It seems the editor must walk the plank.
You'd think that Gray's Inn Road was Watergate.
If driving there you should go in a tank.
The building's angled walls of armour plate
Look harder to bust open than a bank,
But in the corridors strong men now stagger
Their shoulders having grown the sudden dagger.

By having Rupert Murdoch as proprietor
Printing House Square hoped for some meed of peace,
But even if at first the storms grew quieter
From disputation there was no release.
And now your average *Times* man thinks a rioter
Is lucky to be fighting just the police,
Such is the measure of the relaxation
Achieved under the Murdoch dispensation.

When I dispraise my great compatriot
It's not just out of envy for his loot,
Though if it's good he should have such a lot
Still tends to strike me as a point that's moot.
For how his influence sends things to pot,
However, one's concern must be acute.
The centre cannot hold, things fall apart
And everybody ends up in the cart.

Howe's Budget pacifies the Tory Wets,
And at the same time seems fine to the Drys.
In other words, the PM's hedged her bets
If only for the breathing space it buys
While everyone who's got a job forgets
Roy Jenkins once was roughly twice as wise
A Chancellor as is Sir Geoffrey Howe –
A fact she'd rather like suppressed just now.

[183]

The Peace of Bishop's Stortford and Howe's Budget –
In each case the effect might not be meant,
But if it's by the outcome that you judge it
You must ascribe it to the one intent:
Don't rock the party boat or even nudge it,
Bail as a team until the squall is spent,
And when the central threat has blown away
We'll fight among ourselves another day.

At Hillhead Jenkins slips back in the polls.
The press rehearses doom for the Alliance.
Great play is made with the electoral rolls.
Psephology is cried up as a science.
E'en as the cookie crumbles the bell tolls.
The gaff is blown and fate brooks no defiance.
One question, though, if anybody cares:
How often do *you* answer questionnaires?

Never, of course, because you are too bright,
As most Hillheaders are cracked up to be.
Which could just mean, if I am guessing right,
There's still a vote there for the SDP,
Though if it will be all right on the night
We'll simply have to wait ten days and see,
While Jenkins stands increasingly alone
On those cold concave doorsteps of grey stone.

V

Supposedly a media creation,
The SDP's now patronised in print
From all sides as a hollow aberration,
A candy zero like a Polo Mint.
At best such lofty talk's an irritation,
At worst it sets the heart as hard as flint,
But summed up it must prove, if Jenkins conquers,
That stuff about the media was bonkers.

Columbia flames spaceward from the Cape,
Aboard it a glass box of moths and bees.
As Jenkins makes a last lunge for the tape

The press and pollsters are in agonies.
The free-fall moths still buzz in tip-top shape.
The bees just hang there looking hard to please.
Both moths and bees go nowhere in a hurry,
Bees in a sulk and moths in a fine flurry.

So what's the point of effort in that case?
Why didn't old Roy stay home and write books
Instead of pounding through this paper chase,
The sweat of which does little for his looks?
The bees have got the right approach to space:
The moths flap uselessly like fish on hooks . . .
The tension's fearful and one feels no better for
Committing such a thoroughly mixed metaphor.

The die is cast but does not yet lie still
And while it rolls it's hard to count the dots.
The shape of politics for good or ill
Lies in the gift of a few thousand Scots
Of whom a certain element will fill
Their ballot papers in with jokes and blots –
But that's Democracy and worth preserving
Although at times incredibly unnerving.

Roy Jenkins wins and history is made
Or if not made at least it's modified.
The dingbats straight away are on parade
With Benn at his most foam-flecked and pop-eyed,
Saying the SDP has overplayed
Its hand and now must go out with the tide.
Thus King Canute spake as his feet got wetter,
But further up the beach his court knew better.

But now a comic opera interlude
Wins our attention from cosmetic cares.
The generals in the Argentine, though rude
And cruel and prone to giving themselves airs,
Have in the foreign field so far been shrewd,
Confining lunacy to home affairs.
Their latest coup arouses less admonishment
Than universal open-mouthed astonishment.

[185]

The Falkland Islands taken by invasion?
So what's there to invade excepting sheep?
It's no great wonder that on this occasion
The Foreign Office got caught half asleep.
Deuced awkward that the natives are Caucasian
And what is more, we're told, resolved to keep,
Though so far-flung in crude terms of locality,
All ties intact of British nationality.

Storms in a teacup are a sign of spring
And few can take the Falkland business seriously.
Wavers of flags will have their little fling,
Diehard imperialists wil speak imperiously,
And one sincerely trusts that the whole thing
Will fade away the way it came, mysteriously.
Meanwhile by long tradition Oxford's won
The boat race and there's been whole hours of sun.

Dick Saunders at the age of forty-eight
Wins the Grand National. Excellent result.
We raddled crocks excitedly spectate
Dismissing youth as no more than a cult.
The horses nose-dive at a frightful rate.
It's carnage yet one can't help but exult
As David Coleman, fiftyish and cocky,
Congratulates 'the oldest winning jockey'.

Nobody wants to be a fading power
And countries are like men in that regard.
A nation brushed aside as past its hour
Even if that is true will take it hard.
The sceptic courts a sojourn in the Tower
Of London with a yeoman as a guard.
War fever mounts. All one can do is watch it
And hope that this time our side doesn't botch it.

The Secretary of Defence, John Nott,
Has made a whopping balls-up in the House.
The Foreign Secretary's on the spot,
Loudly accused of being short of nous.

The top gun-boat exponent of the lot,
A prancing lion where once crouched a mouse,
Is Michael Foot, who now speaks for the nation
In this alleged Hour of Humiliation.

Lord Carrington presents the dazed PM
With his own head upon a point of honour.
The nitwit Nott stays at his post *pro tem*
Though in the long term he must be a goner.
Poor Thatcher makes a mighty show of phlegm
At all the bad luck that's been heaped upon her,
Announcing, as the Fleet prepares to sail,
We must not even *think* that we might fail.

Such rhetoric is brave if weirdly phrased,
Though fustian it's backed up by legality,
Yet what can't help but leave you slightly fazed
Is the persistent air of unreality.
Those china eyes of hers were always glazed
But now have the glaucoma of fatality,
As if what happened on the field of Mars
Could somehow be predicted by the stars.

Proud ancient Athens sent a sure-fire mission
So strong it could not fail to overawe.
Its name was the Sicilian Expedition.
It lost them the Peloponnesian War.
Ill fortune and long distance worked attrition
Not even the most timorous foresaw.
Thucydides was there and for posterity
Wrote down the consequences of temerity.

As those Greeks at Piraeus in the dawn
Cheered when the galleys raced towards Aegina,
Our patriots now lean on the car horn.
The little motor-boats from the marina
Are teeming in each other's wash like spawn.
All wish the Fleet fair winds for Argentina.
Invincible looks worthy of its name.
The battleship *Repulse* once looked the same.

[187]

I don't doubt our atomic submarines
Can sink their diesel ones in nothing flat.
We sold them all our second-best machines
And man to man should put them on the mat.
But time and place are with the Argentines:
Say what you like there is no blinking that.
We'll take two weeks to get to where we're going –
Which means that until then there's just no knowing.

Two weeks of spring in England, with the hedges
Acquiring flowering hawthorn like dried snow.
The lawns with rows of daffodils at the edges
In Cambridge look too succulent to mow.
I'm told at night they jack them up on wedges
And pull the grass down slightly from below.
Millions of tourists sip at a serenity
Made all the sweeter by the world's obscenity.

Two weeks in the museum and the garden
That some say bitterly Britain's become.
They say Dutch elm disease is rife in Arden.
Britannia's teeth have grown loose in the gum.
The brain gets softer as the arteries harden.
There's too much store set by detached aplomb . . .
So think the vitalists and spoil for action,
Finding in hesitation no attraction.

Two weeks go by and there's no other news
Except what centres on the vexed Malvinas.
If UN Resolution 502's
To mean a thing the next move's Argentina's.
The Yanks, alas, are either short of clues
Or scared of being taken to the cleaners.
Al Haig, while six quacks monitor his ticker,
Sits on the fence through which his allies bicker.

South Georgia falls to us with no life lost.
Our Fleet is justly proud but Fleet Street's prouder.
The jingo hacks want war at any cost:
Abaft cleared desks they perch on kegs of powder.

At last the US gets its wires uncrossed.
Sighs of relief are heaved but somewhat louder
The first bombs fall. It may or may not suit you,
But those who are about to die salute you.

VI

As fifty thousand people in Warsaw
March for Walesa and for Solidarity,
They rate, beside the South Atlantic war,
The same space as a fun run staged for charity.
The Falklands dwarf even El Salvador,
Which ought to be a ludicrous disparity,
But clear-cut issues fought out to a finish
Have sex appeal no slaughter can diminish.

Port Stanley's airstrip is the first thing hurt,
Bombed by a Vulcan and a pack of Harriers.
No skin and hair fly with the grass and dirt.
Unharmed back to Ascension and the carriers
Go all the planes. This war seems snugly girt,
Like some Grand Prix, with crash-proof safety barriers.
It would be fun to watch it on TV
Instead of that chap from the MOD.

You couldn't call the way he talks laconic,
Which mainly means not to be too effusive.
What few words come from this guy are subsonic.
While waiting for the point you grow abusive.
And yet it adds up to a national tonic
For reasons which to my mind prove elusive,
Unless based on a firm belief that God
Speaks to one people and spares them the rod.

Indeed the other side is first to find
Even a sand-tray war costs full-sized lives.
Summoned by noise of a familiar kind
The Exterminating Angel now arrives.
Perhaps, although like Justice he is blind,
It riles him that the gauchos fight with knives:
At any rate, they are the ones he picks
To prove that punctured ships go down like bricks.

[189]

Their cruiser the *Belgrano* takes a hit
Opening up her side to the cold sea,
Which enters in and there's an end of it.
Hundreds of sailors either can't swim free
Or can but freeze, and prayers don't help a bit,
Nor raise the temperature by one degree.
The fire is just to burn those who don't drown
As too full of young voices she goes down.

This is the finest hour of *Mail* and *Star*.
The *Sun* especially is cock-a-hoop,
Shouting commands as if at Trafalgar.
Swab out the trunnion cleats and caulk that poop!
What terrifying warriors they are,
These slewed slop-slingers of the slipshod sloop
El Vino, which each lunchtime takes them south
Into the raging gales of the loud mouth.

A scrivener myself, I should not gripe.
The natural consequence of a free press
Must be that hacks are well paid to write tripe.
One normally feels more scorn than distress
At clichés ready set in slugs of type,
But this exceeds the usual heartlessness:
Faced with a raucous clamour so mind-bending
You wonder if free speech is worth defending.

The war dance falters. Foam dries on the lips
As word by drawn-out word the news comes through:
The *Sheffield*, one of our most modern ships,
A spanking, Sea Dart-armed type 42
Destroyer built to wipe out radar blips,
A Space Invaders expert's dream come true,
Is hit. With what's so far an untold cost
In lives. Has burned. Is given up for lost.

An Etendard released an Exocet
Which duly skimmed the waves as advertised.
Our tabloids wring what mileage they can get
Out of French perfidy, but undisguised

Is their amazement such a classy jet
Flown by these dagoes that they've patronised
Should leave the runway, let alone deliver
This thing so clever that it makes you shiver.

Imagination, if it slept before,
Is now awake and fully occupied
By what's occurred and still might be in store.
With closed eyes you can see the way they died:
The bulkheads hot as a reactor core,
The air the same to breathe as cyanide.
And now that the grim news has got us thinking,
Think of the *Canberra* broken-backed and sinking.

With all at risk there is a pause for thought,
But lest the nation's troubled heart grow faint
El Vino without ever leaving port
Fires paper salvoes that confer the taint
Of Traitor on the doubtful. All those caught
Equivocating must dodge yellow paint
Which flies in dollops like wet chamois leathers
Whilst air-burst cardboard shells disgorge white feathers.

My own view is we ought to go ahead
Even though press support brings only shame.
But my view's that of one with a warm bed
While others face the shrapnel and the flame.
What can you do except note with due dread
The other side in this case are to blame
And would, unless constrained to go away,
Keep what they took though talking till Doomsday?

Such elementary thoughts make me feel dull.
Rarely is it so simple to be right.
But for the nonce there is a blessed lull.
It's possible the UN still just might
Ensure we've seen the last cracked-open hull
And fighter plane turned to a fire in flight.
The mind, robbed of its surfeit of raw action,
Spoiled for the real now searches for distraction.

[191]

Snooker on television is the moral
Equivalent of war. Man against man,
It is a pitiless yet bloodless quarrel
Racking the nerves behind the deadened pan.
Slowly a break accumulates like coral
Yet has the logic of a battle plan.
Fought out on a flat sea within four walls
Well has this conflict been called chess with balls.

This year the final's between two ex-champs.
Veteran Ray Reardon's cool, calm and collected,
While Alex Higgins twitches and gets cramps
Whenever from his headlong rush deflected.
I'd like to keep a foot in both these camps,
Believing the two styles, deep down, connected.
They fight it to a finish frame by frame
And no one doubts it's more than just a game.

Higgins has won and as the fuss subsides
We realise that a game is all it is:
A fish-tank show of strength by fortune's tides,
A show-case for old smoothness and young fizz,
Where Reardon's neatly brushed short back and sides
Bow out with good grace to a lank-haired whizz,
And from the Crucible, their battlefield,
Nobody needs to go home on a shield.

But now on Friday, 21st of May
We hear what happens in a proper fight.
Eight thousand miles south in San Carlos Bay
The invasion has been going on all night.
Men on both sides have really died today.
The bridgehead's been wide open since first light.
Out in the Sound our gun-line ships pump flak
Through which their planes fly low to the attack.

I'm speaking as an armchair strategist
Who's been through every scrap since Marathon
When I suggest (some colleagues would insist)
Amphibious assaults are just not on

[192]

Unless you've got the air clasped in your fist.
This is the biggest gamble since Inchon,
And there the Yanks had more planes than they knew
Quite what to do with. We've got precious few.

Not that the Harrier falls short of being
A modern miracle of engineering.
When it performs you can't grasp what you're seeing:
A frisbee fork-lift truck with power steering,
It floats, flies backwards, stem-turns as if skiing –
The thing's a runabout for Wilma Deering.
The Argentines are suitably outclassed
But still get through by going low and fast.

No pictures except those in the mind's eye
Exist to give some inkling of the scene.
The Skyhawks and Mirages come mast-high,
We're told, but must suppose what those words mean.
Our rockets rush to burst them as they fly
Like thrown milk bottles full of kerosene,
But back along their line of flight the bay
Seeded by bombs grows tall white trees of spray.

So it goes on but can't go on for ever
Without ships hit by something worse than spume.
Brave pilots die in swarms but their endeavour
Is part-rewarded when a bomb finds room
Inside the frigate *Ardent*, there to sever
Her spinal column like a lowered boom.
We're also told they've hit the *Antelope*
But that bomb was a dud and she can cope.

VII

It wasn't. Twenty hours from being struck
The *Antelope* erupts in the dark night.
Having no pictures might be our good luck:
Without doubt it's a mesmerising sight.
The mere sound is enough to make you duck,
But what might really make us choke with fright
Would be to see the troopships the next morning
Still looming there in spite of that grim warning.

Ashore in strength, our soldiers now advance.
The Pope's at Gatwick with the same intention.
It could be said he's taking the same chance
Of getting shot, but let's not even mention
That possibility as the slow dance
Of ritual opens with his condescension
To kiss the tarmac, which this osculation
No doubt excites to transubstantiation.

The Popemobile moves off on its campaign
Of conquest, firing fusillades of prayer.
Appropriate response I find a strain,
Suspecting that this pontiff talks hot air
And only got the part when Michael Caine
Turned cold on the long frocks he'd have to wear.
But thousands of young Catholics seem delighted
As if he were the Beatles reunited.

Without fail every rock-concert-sized crowd
Goes mad while the old boy lays down the law.
It seems that birth control's still not allowed.
Also he deeply disapproves of war.
His fans are all too busy being wowed
To search these propositions for a flaw.
He might as well be singing 'Love me tender'.
They shout and put their hands up in surrender.

Soon now the Argentines will do that too.
Their Skyhawks still punch large holes in our fleet
But in Port Stanley they must know they're through.
The paras and marines slog through the peat
Towards them looking too tough to be true.
A chilling enough spectre of defeat
To make those poor young hungry conscripts wary
About the last stand promised by Galtieri.

Reminding us that it's not over yet
The *Coventry* is lost, and in Bluff Cove
The prospect that has always made one sweat
Comes true. The Skyhawks find their treasure trove:

[194]

A loaded troopship, which they promptly set
Ablaze like a defective petrol stove.
We're given just the name, *Sir Galahad*.
No figures, which suggests they might be bad.

That was the nightmare from the very start,
The sea full of drowned soldiers, but the dread
Is dulled by distance to a thing apart.
Israel's ambassador is left for dead
In London, which one tends to take to heart.
He lies there with a bullet in the head.
Israel strikes north into the Lebanon
And instantly another war is on.

Reagan rides into London looking grey
Around the gills at how the world is going.
By this, of course, I do not mean to say
His make-up's worn off and the real skin's showing:
Just that the outer pancake's flaked away
To show the thick foundation wanly glowing,
Cracked by his smile of disbelief at meeting
Lord Hailsham dressed for the official greeting.

If Reagan's jet-black hair seems slightly strange,
What about Hailsham's wig, sword, socks and cape?
The President when dressed to ride the range
Looks odd, but not as weird as a square grape.
For Reagan it must make at least a change
Wondering how they let this nut escape,
As backwards Hailsham goes with a low bow
Showing him where the boys sit down to chow.

The Falklands war ends and Galtieri falls:
His hawk-like features drawn as a wet sheet,
He takes a minimum of curtain calls
And finds, outside the stage door in the street,
That though his mouth continues to spout balls
His tears have made mud pies of his clay feet,
And so he has to crawl instead of walk
Home to a house full of his empty talk.

One counts the hundreds dead in the Atlantic
And feels regretful at the very least,
But as wars go it rated as romantic
Beside the shambles in the Middle East,
Where thousands are dead, maimed or driven frantic
As round Beirut the steel squeeze is increased.
Some say the Jews have been transmogrified
To Nazis, and that this is Genocide.

One doesn't have to be a Zionist
To spot the weakness in this parallel.
Begin strikes me as still the terrorist
He started off as and a fool as well,
But bad though things now look, one must insist
That war is war. The Holocaust was Hell.
For Begin, children's deaths seem incidental.
For Adolf Hitler they were fundamental.

The Nazis sought complete obliteration,
Women and children being top priority.
The PLO's a warlike armed formation
Whose goal – we have it on their own authority –
Is Israel's disappearance as a nation.
No nonsense about rights for the minority,
Just dumb insistence that the hated state
Should make its mind up to evaporate.

The Jews won't sit still twice for being slaughtered.
The Palestinians will fight to live.
Justice and mercy will be drawn and quartered.
Things will be done a saint could not forgive.
The towns and cities will be bombed and mortared
Until like hot sand they fall through a sieve,
And on the day that blood turns into wine
There will be peace again in Palestine.

My biblical locutions you'll excuse:
The Royal Birth, if not a new Nativity,
Is everywhere regarded as Good News
Except by those of levelling proclivity

[196]

Who think the common folk do not enthuse
At such shows of élitist exclusivity
From choice, but somehow cheer because they've got to,
Being by glamour too bedazzled not to.

War-leader Thatcher. having proved her nerve,
Now rants of a new spirit sweeping Britain,
But peace is not war and high talk won't serve
For long to stop the biter getting bitten.
Let's hope the lorries don't run short of derv:
Even as this last couplet's being written
The London Tube strike's trumped by British Rail,
Which stops dead too but on a larger scale.

A Borgless Wimbledon soaks up the rain
Which falls like a monsoon arriving late.
Al Haig resigns with every sign of strain:
Someone called Shultz is now in charge at State.
The new prince is named William. The odd train
Starts up again as if to celebrate,
But ASLEF thinks a moving train just fosters
Flexible notions with regard to rosters.

Ray Buckton therefore plans a whole new strike.
Meanwhile the members of the SDP
Mark ballot slips to name the man they'd like
To lead them on the stroll to destiny.
The polls and press say Roy will need a bike:
Young Owen's gone too far ahead to see.
Fuelled by the Falklands Factor Owen's flowered
And left Roy looking rather underpowered.

Most members of the SDP, however,
Joined in the first place to see Roy PM.
No question Dr Owen's very clever:
The elder statesman's still the man for them.
They vote to prove the Falklands business never
Made hazy the true *terminus ad quem*.
The thing that matters is the next election,
Not smart young David's feelings of rejection.

[197]

Though disappointed, Owen takes it well.
One might just say the same for McEnroe.
Outplayed by Connors he does not raise hell
But mainly hangs his head in silent woe.
He lurks like a sick crab in a dull shell.
His only tantrum is to drag his toe,
And when a cross-court drive goes nowhere near it
Say 'Fuck it' where the umpire cannot hear it.

Jimbo I've always thought was mighty good.
It's nice to see a champion come back.
But McEnroe, we're told, is such a hood
That when he can't run haywire he goes slack.
He should have smashed his racket to matchwood
And used the jagged handle to attack
The umpire, linesmen, ballboys, Duke of Kent
And so on till his bottled wrath was spent.

For McEnroe, Release of Pent-up Tension
(I quote Mark Cox, player turned commentator)
Is fundamental to the whole dimension
Of polished touch akin to Walter Pater
Which makes John's game so marvellous the mere mention
Of his resemblance to an alligator
Can only mean that genius is beyond us –
Unless, of course, the little bastard's conned us.

VIII

Off home flies McEnroe in deep dejection,
His face a sweet potato cooked in steam.
But this time his behaviour bore inspection,
The usual nightmare merely a bad dream.
One looks upon him almost with affection
And hopes the England World Cup football team
Will similarly take the setback stoically
If it transpires they don't do so heroically.

A goalless draw with Spain wipes out the chance
England was in with. Miffed at how we muffed it,
The British fans, deprived now of romance,

Regain the sad hotels in which they've roughed it
And ponder at great length the fact that France
Was the one team to whom we really stuffed it.
Many a fan's bald head shows the deep crease
Made by the impact of the Spanish police.

Young men of Britain sleep now at Goose Green
In plastic bags lined up in a long grave.
Large speeches were engendered by that scene
Of how our Comprehensive lads were brave.
But now, as if the war had never been,
The thrill is gone and when yobs misbehave
In youthful ways that tend towards the strenuous,
Thatcher's New Spirit looks a trifle tenuous.

A young man penetrates Buck House by night
And duns the Monarch for a cigarette.
It's her behalf on which we all take fright,
Loath to admit the idea makes us sweat
Of some dark whisper asking for a light . . .
But this chill prospect's easily offset,
For though the endless train strike makes you chafe
It means rail travel's absolutely safe.

The man who shook the Queen down for a fag
Is nabbed and named unsmilingly as Fagan.
Though young, it seems he rates as an old lag.
He's got a dossier on him like Lord Kagan.
He's dropped in several times to chew the rag
And strolled around at leisure like Carl Sagan.
An expert on the Palace architecture
Perhaps he wanted her to hear him lecture.

The police, alas, were clueless by comparison.
One of the cops was in bed with a maid.
While as for all that military garrison,
It turns out they do nothing but parade.
You'd think that they might detail the odd Saracen
To park outside her bedroom . . . Feeling frayed,
The Queen perhaps is not best placed to hear
Her personal detective is a queer.

No doubt she sort of sussed but did not mind,
Certain at least the poor klutz wasn't chasing
The tweenies, but now that the clot's resigned
So publicly, it must be less than bracing
For her to know the best men they could find
To guard against the danger that she's facing
From acid, knife, gun, gas, napalm and bomb
Had rings run round them by a peeping Tom.

Foot plumps for ASLEF but as if in spite
The TUC does not and the strike's broken.
Foot's coiffe should go a purer shade of white
Unless his fiery gesture was a token
To make him look a tough nut in a fight
For all those gritty doctrines he has spoken
On that day when they have to be renounced
And Arthur Scargill's strike bid must be trounced.

But Arthur's rhetoric is like his hair.
Though spurious, transparent and bombastic,
It's legal and has some right to be there.
The threat it poses to the State is drastic
But one democracy's equipped to bear.
He's less fanatical than he's fantastic.
That puff-ball pan's so openly ambitious
Only a stocking mask could make it vicious.

Indeed his nimbus of elated strands
Bespeaks not just the patience of a saint
But holiness. It balances no hands.
The halo Giotto botched with thick gold paint
On Arthur's a UFO that never lands,
A cap of gossamer you might find quaint
But can't deny has something brave about it –
He's sparing us the way he'd look without it.

The real and lasting threat to national sanity
Has no objection to remaining nameless.
Among its vices you could not count vanity.
On that score its participants are blameless.

They aim to wake your sense of shared humanity
By perpetrating outrages so shameless
That you will grant a view must have validity
Which gives rise to such murderous stupidity.

In Knightsbridge a car bomb with up-to-date
Remote controls proves powerful competition
For horsemen wearing plumes and silver plate,
While up in Regent's Park a similar mission
Is carried out with a success as great,
Ensuring, at the moment of ignition,
Musicians who have never hurt a soul
Are shown up in their true repressive role.

For what's a bandsman, when all's said and done,
If not a soldier of a certain sort?
What is a trombone but a type of gun?
What is a bandstand but a kind of fort?
Objectively, the difference is none:
These men were troops no matter what they thought,
And as for sleepy listening civilians –
They symbolise the acquiescent millions

Who now unquestionably come awake
And wonder for a week stretched to nine days
If this is not more than the nerves can take.
The horses' wounds bared to the public gaze
Cause many a grave thoughtful head to shake.
Dumb pain is real but how strange that it weighs
Thus heavily, when humans ask what mattered
So much it left them or their loved ones shattered.

Did Cromwell's ruthlessness bring this to pass,
A woman crawling with a face of blood?
Did the Earl of Essex raise a storm of glass
When he set fire to houses of thatched mud?
A bugle boy for being armed with brass
Was pricked to die. What caused that? The Great Flood?
The grievous debt goes back to the beginning
That makes these men more sinned against than sinning.

The guilty live, the innocent lie dead:
The summer sun shines warmly on them all.
In Biarritz it shines on my bald head.
My scalp accepts the photons as they fall.
No Scargill I, I let my skull turn red,
Building my daughters a thick sand sea wall.
They crouch behind it, clinging to the notion
Somehow their father can control the ocean.

I can't stop waves, or much else, reaching them.
Relieved they're not in Belfast or Beirut
I'm flattered in a way some might condemn
To find their sense of beauty so acute.
Each shell's looked at as if it were a gem,
Held to the ear, then blown on like a flute.
By those too young to know the world is cruel
A cured sea-horse is treasured as a jewel.

The London papers bring the usual news –
Inflation's down yet unemployment climbs.
But here the gulf's laid out in greens and blues:
Lapis, fresh lettuce and the juice of limes.
Lulled by the heat, one's body cells refuse
To wait for the return of better times:
They take their holiday though deprivation
Should devastate the luckless British nation.

The spirit's willing but the flesh is weak.
Skin will be free and easy if it can.
Through down-turned mouth with deep concern we speak:
The epidermis has its selfish plan
To look less like the thick end of a leek.
The height of its ambition is a tan.
For two weeks while the tide goes up and down
I watch it and react by turning brown.

In Biarritz the sun sets like a peach
That ripens and ignites towards the water.
Waves which were blue like denims when they bleach
Turn silver as a newly minted quarter.

[202]

Absorbed by darkness outwards from the beach,
Like lemon ice licked by my younger daughter
White light is ineluctably consumed,
Ripples erased. Desired and therefore doomed.

Something fulfilled this hour, loved or endured –
A line of Auden's that burns in the mind.
By now just like the sea-horse I am cured.
Having acquired a dark and brittle rind,
I feel resigned again, if not inured,
To how the real world out there is unkind,
As flying back to it I read Camus
Amazed how he continues to come true.

The innocent, he once wrote, in our age
Must justify themselves. That still sounds right.
The Jews in Paris now take centre-stage.
A restaurant is reamed with gelignite.
The elders might express old-fashioned rage
But modern anti-Semites are more polite,
Claiming that Zionism must be fought
Wherever Jews might offer it support.

Thus reason the Jew-baiters of the Left
As once the Right spoke in *Je suis partout*.
The warp's formed by the same thread as the weft:
Woven together, they are what they do.
Between them there's no fundamental cleft,
A fact appreciated by Camus
Whom both sides honoured with their deepest hate –
In my view a most enviable fate.

IX

In Britain the health workers strike for pay
Which surely in all conscience they've got coming.
The harvest's in and farmers stack the hay.
Around the rotting fruit the wasps are humming.
The CBI says Thatcher must give way.
It's all so soothing, not to say benumbing.
England is now and history is elsewhere.
Most of the rough stuff isn't here, it's there.

[203]

It's there in Israel where General Sharon
Even by Begin's found intransigent.
In Gdansk the water cannon are turned on
As if cold spit could wash away cement.
Now Arafat with all his options gone
Concedes perhaps it's time his people went.
The PLO might recognise Israel.
The Poles pretend Walesa's not in gaol.

But history here at home is the two Krays
Let out of clink to mourn their saintly mother.
The boys for all their rough-and-tumble ways
Both loved her as they never loved another.
People repaired with grafts, pins, splints and stays
Still can't decide which was the nicer brother –
The Kray who'd chat you up before he grabbed you
And held you helpless, or the Kray who stabbed you.

The other big event is Poet Sue,
A scribbling Cambridge undergraduette,
Who as the French once went mad for Minou.
Is cried up as the greatest talent yet
By dons who should have better things to do,
You might think, than to stand there getting wet
Drooling about the girl's supreme facility
For sonnets of Shakespearean fertility.

It seems she churns them out like a machine
That manufactures plastic souvenirs,
And on the whole that's roughly what they mean:
They're so banal you can't believe your ears.
They echo everything that's ever been
Created in the last five hundred years.
Sue's poor brain is a boneyard, a Sargasso,
A pulping mill, a collage by Picasso.

The dons who praise her were once Leavisites,
Slow to admire and vicious in dismissal.
What aberration has brought on these flights
Of rapture as they cluster round a thistle

And call the thing a rose and spend their nights
Composing articles that make you whistle,
Since even Leavis's worst panegyrics
For Ronald Bottrall didn't sound like lyrics?

The dons are punished for their dereliction
With dour gibes from the joyless Donald Davie
Who demonstrates at length Sue's vaunted diction
Tastes thin compared with dehydrated gravy,
While as for her alleged powers of depiction . . .
The dons must feel they've been shelled by the Navy.
He calls them symptoms of a deep malaise
As Cambridge English falls on evil days.

But dons were ever shaky in their taste.
Davie himself is nuts for Ezra Pound.
It's not on judgment their careers are based.
They tend the fields but they break no new ground.
Old Leavis thought that writers could be 'placed'
Even while they still lived and moved around.
Alas, he was so tone-deaf that his scrutiny
Made spinning poets in their graves plot mutiny.

The reason why the dons find Sue prodigious
Is patent when you see a photograph.
No wonder they forgot to be prestigious:
The girl's so pretty that she makes you laugh.
I trust no don involved will get litigious
For being likened to a love-sick calf –
I understand completely how the urge'll
Emerge to call a virgin a new Virgil.

A summer madness that began in spring
The Sue Affair's explained by a don's life.
His winter schedule is a humdrum thing
And often the same goes for the don's wife.
Though every day the sweet girl students bring
Their essays which he goes through like a knife,
The whole deal's on the intellectual level
And busy hands do no work for the Devil.

[205]

But then the crocus drives up to the sun
And Sue puts on a floating cotton dress
And that fine friendship as of priest and nun
Erupts into a secular distress.
Those sonnets that she turns out by the ton
Must mean the girl's a gifted poetess:
Sue's such a doll she'd make Professor Carey
Say that she wrote like Dante Alighieri.

Sue's bubble reputation having popped
Her teachers must wipe soap out of their eyes,
But one would hate to see those young wings cropped
Merely because her mentors were not wise.
If that compulsive gush of hers is stopped
It ought to be because she's learned to prize
The disciplines that temper and anneal,
Growing slow blooms of strength inside the steel.

There's energy in Sue's headlong slapdash
Which most of our young careful craftsmen lack.
They watch their language and do nothing rash.
Crushed in the boot and wound tight on the rack,
Pressed thin with weights and strung up for the lash,
Each poem is a puzzle that won't crack,
Yielding its meaning drop by anguished drop
Until, drained dry, it dies with a full stop.

One image per two stanzas is the ration,
Though some there are who don't risk even that.
Such level surfaces are hard to fashion.
It takes a kind of built-in thermostat
To ward off sudden puffs of wayward passion
Which might cause pimples in what should be flat,
Protected in all possible directions
Against the threat of critical objections.

Better to write in quite another style
And be accused of sentimental clowning.
Better to court the condescending smile
Of that drear ghost still droning on in Downing.

In Italy for all too short a while
I grapple with the greatest work of Browning.
What chance would it have stood against those wits
Of our day whose chief skill is to pick nits?

But even Browning sweated for more density
Than line could hold which brain could still retain.
Astonished by the man's sustained intensity
I see the packed force of that hardwood grain,
But find his parquetry's compressed immensity
Undone by a pervading sense of strain:
The book runs such tight rings around itself
No wonder it sits heavy on the shelf.

Perhaps there's now no hope of being clear
Unless one's also hopelessly naive;
An air of easiness is bought too dear
If cheap effects are all it can achieve;
But in Ferrara I stand very near
The kind of art in which I can believe –
That generous tribute to a mean employer,
Cossa's great frescoes in the Schifanoia.

Faded to pastel they're still full of light.
Each panel has an effortless proportion.
It's love of life that makes those faces bright.
The skill is consummate without distortion.
Sure of its knowledge like a bird in flight,
Such perfect freedom feels no need of caution,
And so the teeming polychrome quotidian
Enjoys perpetually its just meridian.

But just only as art. Injustice then,
As rank as now, had no redress at all.
Below those stately dames and lolling men
A Jew sprints for his life across the wall,
Insistently reminding you of when,
In recent days still well within recall,
So many innocent were naked runners
Towards the mass graves and the machine-gunners.

[207]

X

The past gives solace and rededication
But offers no escape from harsh reality.
Back in the present, all one's information
Suggests the air of gracious informality
The Quattrocento brought to relaxation
Would now seem strained whatever the locality –
There are no independent city-states
Equipped to keep the world outside their gates.

From West Beirut into the waiting ships
The PLO pulls out on television.
With gestures of one cashing in his chips
According to some tactical decision
Their leader puckers those unlovely lips,
But only fools would whistle in derision
As his sad captains all get kissed goodbye –
Mere military defeat won't stop *that* guy.

I must say he's no oil-painting, Yasser,
Or if he is then it's of something weird.
Nothing would make him look as good as Nasser
But still you'd think he'd try a *proper* beard.
For head-gear an entire antimacassar
Arranged so that his features disappeared
Would do more than that tea-towel does at present
To make his aspect generally more pleasant.

One day no doubt he will be played on screen
By some young ringer for Alain Delon.
Most people look at odds with what they mean:
We're bound to simplify them when they're gone.
Golda Meir's reported to have been
Transformed by Ingrid Bergman to a swan,
But now, with Bergman dead at sixty-five,
No one in *Casablanca*'s left alive.

It was a clumsy film with a bum script
Yet watching it once more I sit and dream.
The cigarettes they smoke aren't filter-tipped.

[208]

Bogie pours whisky in a steady stream.
Small vices. It's by virtue they are gripped.
Of self-indulgence there is not a gleam.
She wavers but he has the strength of ten
As time goes by and Sam plays it again.

Reagan and Thatcher ought to be like that.
Instead they have a frightful falling-out.
The Russian pipeline has inspired the spat,
Or that's what spokesmen *say* it's all about.
In private Maggie's spitting like a cat.
In public, as per usual, she says nowt,
Calling the USA our greatest friend
While thinking its top man the living end.

Scargill and Benn say let's break Tebbit's law.
Jim Callaghan less bluntly says that too.
Israel and Syria might go to war.
The boggled mind wonders what else is new.
In Berne the Polish Embassy's front door
Is opened while some breakfast is pushed through:
The terrorists are hauled out bearing traces
Of the omelette which has blown up in their faces.

But wait a second. Don't you find it odd
So dumb a move comes from pro-liberal Poles?
Are these a self-selected awkward squad
Or has the other side smartly switched roles?
To keep Walesa endlessly in quod
It might help if more tender-hearted souls
Thought *Solidarnosc* meant armed insurrection
Against the Party's warm clasp of affection.

It's possible one's getting paranoid:
Walesa's just too big to disappear.
But murder's been a frequently employed
Political technique in this past year.
To show the Government what to avoid
Sicilian *mafiosi* arouse fear
By gunning down the General sent to face them
Before he even gets a chance to chase them.

Dalla Chiesa's death convinces me –
I think that all in all and on the whole
I won't go righting wrongs in Sicily.
Nor will a few lines praising a brave Pole
Do very much to set his people free.
Perhaps a phantom quest's the one sane goal –
As now the *Sun* claims to have found Lord Lucan
In deepest jungle with tapir and toucan.

The Jungle Fugitive's a Fleet Street thriller
That Martin Bormann starred in last time round.
Embezzler on the lam and missing killer
Swathed in lianas are abruptly found.
One day no doubt they'll bump into Glenn Miller,
So many scribes are covering the ground.
He'll be with Harold Holt and all the rest
Back to the crew of the *Marie Celeste*.

No news is good news and fake news is fun
Or would be if the bad news caused less strain.
To stop us laughing too long at the *Sun*
Another DC10 comes down in Spain.
The Lebanon's Gemayel lived by the gun.
He puts the gun down and is promptly slain,
While in her palace chapel Princess Grace
Too soon lies dead in high-necked silk and lace.

Our big affair was over years ago
And merits no more than this brief report.
I claimed her for my own in *Rear Window*
And from the Odeon walked lost in thought
The long way home exuding love's hot glow.
Believing Rainier was far too short,
I gave her up in fury mixed with grief
The seventh time I saw *To Catch a Thief*.

Flying above Beirut towards Bombay
By night en route to faraway Peking
One's well aware that earlier today
Down there the corpses were still quivering.

The most the Israelis are prepared to say
Is that the Christians had their little fling
Unsupervised, with awkward consequences
For Muslims not equipped with barbed-wire fences.

Thousands of blameless people lying dead,
The State of Israel's credit well-nigh wrecked,
And all of it on Begin's bullet head
Who should have seen his duty to protect
Civilian lives if his invasion led
To the point where each and every local sect
Was tempted to vent pent-up animosity
By staging the odd small-scale mass atrocity.

The least that Begin and Sharon can do
Is step down and donate their brains to science.
What few friends Israel has left urge them to
But neither hero seems moved to compliance.
The Knesset is a Hebrew hullabaloo,
The blunderers are childish in defiance,
But for the nonce I put off shame and pity
Standing entranced in the Forbidden City.

For Mrs Thatcher's visit the Chinese
Have laid on a Grade Three official greeting.
Which doesn't mean the bum's rush or the freeze:
She gets an honour guard at the first meeting.
But not much bunting flutters in the breeze.
Tian'anmen Square contains no special seating.
Instead there is a lot of open space
With here and there a mildly curious face.

She's here to pin them down about Hong Kong.
She'd like to have a written guarantee.
The PM's habit is to come on strong.
The Chinese instinct is to wait and see.
Any idea the business won't take long
Ebbs when the welcome turns out so low key.
China in that respect remains immutable –
The people speak Chinese and look inscrutable.

[211]

The great Hall of the People is the venue
For a fifteen-course State Banquet every night.
There isn't any need to read the menu: .
You take a pinch of everything in sight.
It all tastes at least wonderful and when you
Happen upon a dish that's sheer delight
Just go on eating while they bring you more.
They'll keep that up until you hit the floor.

Shown how by locals in black Beatles suits
We find out what to chew and what to suck.
First having added sauce and onion shoots
We fold the pancake round the Peking Duck.
Maddened by fish lips and sliced lotus roots
The journalists eat like a rugby ruck.
Even our diplomats up there with Her
Tuck in so fast their chopsticks are a blur.

A thousand million ordinary Chinese
Are outside staunchly doing what they're told.
They'd never even dream of meals like these.
It's luxury for them just to grow old.
From dawn to dusk the streets swarm with belled bees.
I hire a bike and join them, feeling bold
And bulking large against the average male
As if I were a wobbly, two-wheeled whale.

Petite they are and easy on the eye,
This quarter of the world's whole population.
The same seems even more true in Shanghai.
Each city stuns you like a whole new nation.
They march together under a red sky
Towards a dream of human transformation.
It's awe-inspiring yet one has to say
One's heart goes out still to the Student Wei.

Young Wei it was who, raised as a Red Guard,
Looked back on his achievements with remorse.
With Mao set to cash in his Party card
Deng and the boys announced a change of course.

The Student Wei invited ten years hard
Saying they'd got the cart before the horse:
If freedom came first, progress might begin.
He pulled his ten years and five more thrown in.

XI

If only freedom had a sharper taste.
In Hong Kong kneeling by my father's grave
It's not of his life I regret the waste
But my life he kept safe by being brave.
Even in slavery he was not disgraced,
But self-reproach goes through me like a wave
For all the precious daylight I let spill
While he lies tightly locked in that steep hill.

As Thatcher's VC10 with me aboard
Spears up and doubles westward from Kai Tak
At 30,000 feet I still feel floored
By China and make large plans to go back.
It wasn't Communism I adored:
It was the beauty too refined to crack
From history's hammer blows, and yet possessed
In common, everywhere made manifest.

I never knew the sky was full of dust
Above Peking and turned plum at sunset
While all the palace roofs acquired a crust
Of crumbling honeycomb. If I forget
The details or confuse them as one must,
That first sigh of assent is with me yet.
In China though the mind recoils offended
One's visual range can't help but be extended.

With due allowances, the same's applied
To local artists since the Shang at least.
No bronze bell has been cast or silk bolt dyed
If not with reference to the visual feast
Spread out what still must seem the whole world wide
Each day that dawns where else but in the East?
A boundlessness which suffers no real border
Except the outline of an ideal order.

[213]

Sung pictures fix my dreams of public art:
Intensely subtle, spaciously compact,
Produced by an élite not set apart,
The theory left implicit in the fact,
A measured naturalness felt from the heart,
The intellect controlled by natural tact –
Schooled to the limit yet prepared to meet
Halfway the average cyclist in the street.

The cyclist, one need hardly add, sees few
Fine paintings from one year's end to the next,
But still the small extent to which his view
Of local architecture has been vexed
By modern public buildings must be due
To precepts found in no official text,
And least of all in Mao's Little Red Book –
Which you can't buy however hard you look.

Yes, Mao has been reduced from god to man.
He's back to being ordinary flesh.
His mausoleum's small extractor fan
Must now work overtime to keep him fresh.
The Party's cranking out a whole new plan
In which, they say, the word and deed will mesh.
Good luck to them and let's hope Wei gets sprung
In time to share the wealth while he's still young.

We've flown so far that distances deceive
But back in the real world we left behind
The demonstrators march through Tel Aviv.
Sharon and Begin still have not resigned,
But ask their best young people to believe
They never had a massacre in mind.
It must be true since who'd be such a klutz?
Which leaves you thinking they must both be nuts.

There's uproar in the Bundesrepublik
As Schmidt's brought down. Some say he'll get back in
Stronger than ever, others he's so weak
There's just no chance that he can save his skin.

These latter prove correct. Schmidt's up the creek
Without a paddle and Herr Kohl must win.
All those refreshed by Schmidt's astringent attitude
Must now adapt to Kohl's gift for the platitude.

Though Kohl's arrival means there's one bore more
The nett effect seems no worse than narcosis.
We know from sub-Orwellian folklore
That bombast by a process of osmosis
Corrupts the social fabric to the core,
That rhetoric is verbal halitosis –
And yet one still tends to be more afraid
Of forthright men who call a spade a spade.

In Rome some group propounding the belief
That baiting Jews is simply common sense
Creates the optimum amount of grief
By firing shots at minimal expense
Into a crowd of worshippers. Though brief
The sense of satisfaction is intense:
Just one dead child can seem like a whole lot
When that's the only pogrom that you've got.

You know just where you are with men like these.
They say they want to kill you and they mean it.
In Ireland when they nail you through the knees
You know they've got a point because you've seen it.
Be grateful there are no more mysteries:
Thugs hold the slate and you must help them clean it.
You wanted honest politics? They're here.
Answer the door. What have you got to fear?

In Poland where all terror's state-controlled
The time for Solidarity has come
To be outlawed. Leaders left in the cold
Until their lips turned purple and tongues numb
In dribs and drabs are let loose to grow old
As proof it's wiser to be deaf and dumb
When there's few friends outside to be inspired
And room for them inside if so desired.

[215]

But though the days are quicker to grow dark
In Europe now the year starts bowing out,
The flow of dreadful news lifts up an ark
Of hope as all good men combine to shout
Hosannahs for Prince Andrew and Koo Stark,
Who when the chips are down are not in doubt
That what needs doing when the world looks bleak
Is best done on the island of Mustique.

Too bad that jealous Fleet Street crabs the act.
Andrew deserves a break with his show-stopper,
In view of all the dreary weeks he hacked
Around the Falklands with his lonely chopper.
Nevertheless you have to face the fact
Young Koo's the next thing to a teenybopper:
Highly unsuitable and, if adorable
From certain angles, all the more deplorable.

Page Three pin-ups and skin-flick clips of Koo
Are dug out so the Palace might take note
That Koo viewed in the long term just won't do
Though in the short term she would stun a stoat.
We're told the Queen has carpeted Andrew
And warned him not to act the giddy goat.
How do the papers get this information?
Let's hope not by nocturnal infiltration.

Gdansk erupts but Martial Law's imposed
To boost the standard military rule.
The Lenin Shipyard wound is not quite closed
But treatment nowadays is prompt if cruel.
The Zomos leave the area well hosed
With noxious matter flushed down the cesspool.
When Jaruzelski reads the fever chart
He'll see the outbreak stymied at the start.

At home the NUR's lost Sidney Weighell.
The SDP has lost points in the polls.
For parties needing TV time I feel
It's mad to have a Conference that Rolls

Instead of staying put, while the appeal
Of packing up each night as for the hols
Is hard to see, unless they're taking pains
To prove that Shirley Williams can catch trains.

More serious than polls for the Alliance,
Roy's Statutory Incomes Policy
Is greeted with a vote of non-compliance,
Thus demonstrating that the SDP
Is not just for a gang of famous giants
But ordinary folk like you and me –
Stout thinking, yet the move, if not divisive,
Can't help at this stage seeming indecisive.

But John De Lorean shows more than strain
In several parts of that uplifted face.
The handcuffs induce shame on top of pain
As in Los Angeles he falls from grace.
Busted with many kilos of cocaine
Packed neatly in a custom pig-skin case,
He's proved his gull-winged dream car always flew
On snowy puffs of powder from Peru.

And there but for the grace of God go I
Who also in an excess of belief
Am swept up in wild schemes that I swear by
And feel the impact when they come to grief.
But then the raucous critical outcry
Condemns one as more mountebank than thief,
Unless one deals with state funds like De Lorean
And fiddles them like Sallust the historian.

The artist when he claims the Right to Fail
Just means the risk he takes is a sure bet.
Success occurs on an eternal scale.
The lack of it we instantly forget.
The man of action's not free to avail
Himself of such a useful safety net:
He bites the sawdust with the floodlights shining.
The crowd stays put to watch the vultures dining.

[217]

XII

A fact which Arthur Scargill demonstrates
By calling on his membership to strike.
Most of the men down mines are Arthur's mates –
He fights on their behalf and that they like,
However much his bumptious manner grates –
But now they tell him to get on his bike.
From lower chin to fairy-floss beret
His visage holds more egg than a soufflé.

You'd almost think 'poor Arthur' were it not
That Solidarity's new riots show
How little chance a free trade union's got
Once fear is planted and has time to grow.
There's no need nowadays to fire a shot.
Just make them run. They've got nowhere to go.
The hoses gush, the truncheons rise and fall
And where a thousand marched, a hundred crawl.

The movement is just two years old today
And looks already paralysed with age.
That fine collective courage drains away
Into a helpless, inward-turning rage.
The price of protest gets too high to pay.
You shake the bars but cannot shift the cage.
Only the young can be brave as they wish
When one-time physicists are selling fish.

Atomic bombs are our first-string defence
Against all this. A reassuring sign
Is that they're backed up by Intelligence:
From GCHQ any foe's phone line
In two ticks can be tapped at his expense.
A man employed there says it works just fine,
And if he sounds a trifle well-rehearsed
It's just because he told the Russians first.

One secret, though, the Russians couldn't keep
A moment longer even if they tried.
Brezhnev might well be more than just asleep.
It's reasonably certain he has died.

The time has come for crocodiles to weep
And stir the bucket of formaldehyde.
The last spark has winked out in that great brain
Which once did Stalin's work in the Ukraine.

Andropov of the KGB emerges
Inevitably as the next big cheese.
In Hungary he supervised the purges
Which taught them just how hard the Bear can squeeze.
But now it seems he has artistic urges
And intellectual proclivities.
At speaking English he is Leslie Howard:
At playing the piano, Noel Coward.

There's consolation in a fairy-tale,
But none when Lech Walesa is released –
Surely the final proof that he must fail.
In back rooms as a species of lay priest
He might say mass but only in a pale
Reflection of that sacrificial feast
When Poland at the hour of dedication
Tasted what life is like in a free nation.

In Congress Reagan loses the MX
Because they don't think much of the Dense Pack –
A grand scheme calculated to perplex
Red rockets as they swoop to the attack.
Them critters will collide and break their necks.
Some will run wild and others will head back
To blow the roof off the Politburo.
Remember John Wayne and the Alamo!

But there will be, should our blue planet burn,
At least some shred of reason for the fire;
There's just no guarantee we'd ever learn,
Try as we might, to live behind barbed wire;
So threat and counter-threat, though they might turn
The stomach, are not terminally dire –
Although we say it sitting in a crater
The aim was to talk first instead of later.

[219]

Someone thinks otherwise in Ballykelly.
A pub explodes and falls on those inside.
The whole platoon of soldiers blown to jelly
Must constitute a cause for secret pride.
Those girls who should have been home watching telly
You'd have to say committed suicide,
An act which no true Christian can condone.
So ends the news-flash from the battle zone.

Ken Livingstone has failed to uninvite
The IRA to meet the GLC.
The Fleet Street hacks with ill-concealed delight
Pour hot lead on his inhumanity.
I like his gall but question his eyesight.
When looking at his newts what does he see?
You'd think that his pop eyes could count their eggs.
No doubt he'd spot it if *they* lost their legs.

In Florida the last month of the year
Is balmier than England was in June.
There's wild hogs in the boondocks around here
And manatees asleep in the lagoon.
Launch Complex 39's the stack of gear
That fired the first Apollo at the Moon.
Beside Pad A the storks pose poised to scuttle
At any sign of life from the Space Shuttle,

Which stands on end all set to hit the trail
Out of this charnel house that we inhabit.
It's an ejector seat on a world scale.
Given just half a chance who wouldn't grab it?
Sit still for the volcano up your tail
And you'd be off and running like a rabbit –
Till upside down, a baby before birth,
Floating in silence you would see the Earth.

Earth shows no signs of us viewed from up there
Except the Wall of China, so no wonder
It looks a vision in its veils of air,
The white opacities we hear as thunder

Braided with azure into maidenhair –
It's those conditions we are living under.
That stately clockwork of soft wheels and springs
Keeps time whatever mess we make of things.

Back in the London frost I pile up drifts
Of crumpled A4 as I type my piece.
Some halfwit has been spitting in the lifts.
The thieves patrol more often than the police.
I head for Cambridge with the children's gifts,
Walk down a street made loud by sizzling geese
And am appropriately stunned to see
The work continues on our Christmas tree.

An angel where there used to be a star.
Twin tinsel strings like stage-struck DNA.
The leaves peel off the Advent calendar
Uncovering one chocolate every day.
The decorators may have gone too far
In hanging Santa Claus from his own sleigh.
Behold two members of the privileged class –
The young, who think that time will never pass.

Too soon to tell them, even if I knew,
The secret of believing life is good
When all that happened was the scythe spared you
While better men were cut down where they stood.
My fortunes thrived in 1982.
I'd have it on my conscience if I could,
But next year will be time to make amends
For feeling happy as the old year ends.

[221]